GUIDED FLIGHT DISCOVERY
PRIVATE PILOT
SYLLABUS

Cover Photos
Diamond airplane in flight courtesy of Diamond Aircraft Industries

ISBN 978-0-88487-171-2

Jeppesen
55 Inverness Drive East
Englewood, CO 80112-5498
Web site: www.jeppesen.com
Email: Captain@jeppesen.com
Copyright © Jeppesen
All Rights Reserved.
Published 1997, 2002, 2007, 2012, 2015, 2016
10001292-004

Preface

The Private Pilot Syllabus meets the requirements of 14 CFR, Part 141. This syllabus refers to 14 CFR parts and regulations as Federal Aviation Regulations (FARs). The syllabus is an outline, or map, for the course of training. Instructors should also refer to the pertinent sections of the regulations when teaching the course to ensure that no aeronautical knowledge areas, flight proficiency, or experience requirements are omitted during pilot training and that they are documented in appropriate records. The terminology for maneuvers and procedures listed in the syllabus is aligned with the tasks that are published in the FAA's *Private Pilot Airman Certification Standards*.

The Syllabus has separate ground and flight training courses that are designed to be taught concurrently. The Ground Training Syllabus is divided into three stages and contains a total of 17 ground lessons. The Flight Training Syllabus also is divided into three stages and contains a total of 26 flight lessons. A stage *check* is included at the end of each stage of *flight* training, and a stage *exam* is included at the end of each stage of *ground* training. A presolo knowledge exam is included before the first supervised solo. In addition, end-of-course knowledge exams and an end-of-course flight check are included in the syllabus prior to the conclusion of the respective ground and flight segments. The End-of-Course Flight Check is completed at the end of Stage III. The applicant must complete, or receive credit for, all of the ground and flight lessons in the *Private Pilot Syllabus*.

Computer-assisted training is incorporated into this syllabus as follows:
- The Private Pilot Online training course in the Jeppesen Learning Center
  ◊ Ground Lessons
  ◊ Maneuvers Lessons
- An aviation training device (ATD) for specified ground lessons

To accommodate the requirements of some flight schools, this syllabus offers the option of conducting the Stage I Check prior to the first solo flight. If operators want to incorporate this flight lesson sequence or utilize an aviation training device, they should check the appropriate boxes below when applying for training course outline (TCO) approval and mark the student copy of the syllabus.

❑ This syllabus has the Stage I Check (Flight Lesson 10) preceding the first solo (Flight Lesson 9).
❑ This syllabus utilizes an ATD in the ground training segment.

_____ is enrolled in the Private
(Name)   Pilot Certification Course.

Table of Contents

Introduction

This syllabus utilizes the building-block method of teaching in which each instructional item is presented on the basis of previously learned knowledge and skill. It guides students and instructors through a lesson sequence in which new material builds on what a student has already mastered.

HOW TO PRESENT
THE JEPPESEN PRIVATE PILOT COURSE

The Private Pilot Course contains separate ground and flight training courses, enabling you to teach the ground school separately, as aviation colleges often do. But for schools that have the flexibility, following the recommended lesson sequence shown in the time allocation tables interleaves the ground and flight lessons in a way that enables aeronautical knowledge pertinent to a flight lesson to be taught just before that flight.

THE GROUND TRAINING COURSE

FAR Part 141 considers ground school training to be an integral part of pilot certification courses. This syllabus supports this requirement.

When coordinating the ground school with flight training, each ground lesson is conducted at the point indicated in the Lesson Time Allocation tables beginning on page xvii. Ground training Stages I and II are completed during Stage I of the flight training syllabus. Ground Stage III, and the End-of-Course Final Exams "A" and "B" are completed during Stage II of flight training. This enables the student to complete the aeronautical knowledge segments of the syllabus early before the final stage of flight training, and it encourages the student to take the FAA Private Pilot Airman Knowledge Test at an opportune time.

When the ground training course is presented in a classroom environment, lessons should normally be presented in numerical order. However, to provide some flexibility for adapting to individual student needs and to the training situation, the order of the lessons may be altered with approval of the chief flight instructor. Any deviation should not disturb the course continuity or objectives. Each lesson may be presented in one classroom session, or it may be divided into two or more sessions, as necessary.

GROUND TRAINING COMPONENTS

Jeppesen's *Guided Flight Discovery* (GFD) Pilot Training System provides everything you need to effectively train for a private pilot certificate. Students and instructors should review the following list as a guide to assemble and use the Jeppesen course materials to best advantage.

Private Pilot Syllabus

This syllabus is the map of your Private Pilot course. Study this syllabus to learn what students need to study, and where they go to find what they need to study.

The Jeppesen Private Pilot textbook, also available as an eBook for a tablet computer, is the authoritative source for student study and review. Ground lessons in this syllabus are built on reading assignments from the textbook. The Private Pilot textbook is the essential reference for the aeronautical knowledge every pilot needs and yet is fun and easy to read, relevant, and generously illustrated. Look at the front of the book to learn how it is organized and gain the most advantage from the extraordinary learning tools the book offers.

The Jeppesen Learning Center Online is computer-assisted training (CAT) that provides aeronautical knowledge and maneuvers instruction for your private pilot study. The Private Pilot online course is an extremely effective aid for students to learn on their own or in combination with classroom training. It complements the textbook by presenting the aeronautical principles as an instructor would, including carefully-designed media that helps students better understand the textbook content. Students then see how they are doing with online practice opportunities and exams.

The Jeppesen FAR/AIM, also available as an eBook, is a compilation of appropriate federal aviation regulations (FARs) together with the Aeronautical Information Manual (AIM). The FAR/AIM is updated at least annually. Students need to know this information in addition to the aeronautical knowledge that is presented in the textbook and online course.

Stage exams, end-of-course exams, and the Private Pilot Pre-Solo Written exam are essential training components. All are required for students training under 14 CFR Part 141, and the Pre-Solo Written exam is also required under Part 61. Refer to this syllabus for the timing of these exams.

Jeppesen FAA test guides help students prepare for the FAA private pilot airmen knowledge and practical tests—a guide is available for each of these tests. The private pilot FAA knowledge test guide contains answers and explanations for the FAA airplane test questions. The practical test guide contains guidance for passing the oral portion of the private pilot practical test.

Jeppesen maneuvers training helps private pilot students prepare to practice the skills they must demonstrate in flight. This syllabus recommends specific maneuvers lessons as study assignments for specific flight lessons. Although you can gain approval for a private pilot course that does not use these maneuvers training tools, these assets will save training time by helping students fly a maneuver correctly the first time, and reducing the time required for preflight briefing of maneuvers. The following maneuvers training tools are available:

- **The Private Pilot Maneuvers Manual** provides illustrated step-by-step instructions for all required flight maneuvers, with key knowledge required to perform each maneuver.

- **Online Maneuvers Lessons** are part of the Private Pilot Course in Jeppesen Learning Center. These lessons provide step-by-step guidance with in-cockpit video showing what the pilot sees when performing each maneuver.

INTRODUCTION ■ Private Pilot Course

- **The Private Pilot Video Series on DVD** has maneuvers lessons on Disc 3 that show air-to-air video of essential maneuvers with key knowledge and step-by-step guidance.

- The **Flight Maneuvers Illustrator** is a spiral bound index card size instructional aid that instructors can use in the cockpit to quickly review the required steps and techniques.

LESSON EXAMS

Each ground lesson has a brief exam at the end. Students may complete the exam online in the Jeppesen Learning Center or complete the questions in the appropriate textbook chapter. The exams must be scored and the student must discuss any incorrect responses with the instructor, as specified in the completion standards of a ground lesson. This ensures student understanding prior to beginning the next ground lesson. When a lesson is complete, the instructor assigns the next textbook chapter and section(s) or online lesson(s) for out-of-class study.

STAGE EXAMS

At the end of each stage, the student is required to successfully complete the stage exam outlined in the syllabus before the beginning the next ground training stage. You will find the stage exams in ground lessons 6, 10, and 15. The stage exam evaluates the student's understanding of the knowledge areas within a stage. Successful completion of each stage exam and a review of each incorrect response is required before the student progresses to the next stage.

END-OF-COURSE FINAL EXAMS

When all of the ground lesson assignments are complete, the student should take the End-of-Course Final Exams in ground lessons 16 and 17 of Stage III. Exam "A" is in Lesson 16 and Exam "B," which is ground Lesson 17, serves as the ground training course final examination. Following the exam, the instructor should assign each student appropriate subject areas for review. After a thorough review, the student should complete the FAA *Private Pilot Airman Knowledge Test* without delay.

USING AN ATD FOR GROUND TRAINING

Although you may *not* use an aviation training device (ATD) for any flight training in a private pilot course, the syllabus does provide for use of an ATD for ground training. An ATD is extremely effective for introducing procedures without the distraction of having to fly the airplane. If properly integrated into the ground training program, the ATD will enhance systems knowledge and procedural understanding by the applicant before engaging in flight training in the airplane.

In addition to skill enhancement, the introduction of maneuvers and procedures by instrument reference in the ATD has other advantages for both student and instructor. These include fewer distractions, more versatility in lesson presentation, repositioning, freeze functions, emergency training, and the ability to control the environment of the training session and allow the student to concentrate on the areas the instructor wants to emphasize. By following the recommended sequence of the syllabus, the student will gain maximum benefit from the integration of academic training, introduction of new maneuvers and procedures in the ATD, and subsequent practice in the airplane. The following ground lessons are particularly suited to use of an ATD.

Ground Lesson 1 — Introduction to Aviation   (1 Hour)

Ground Lesson 2 — Airplane Systems   (1 Hour)

Ground Lesson 5 — Communications   (1 Hour)

Ground Lesson 12 — Navigation   (1 Hour)

Ground Lesson 14 — Flying the Cross-Country   (1 Hour)

If the box for ATD utilization is checked on the Preface page, then the ATD becomes part of the ground training segments for the approved course, and its use is required. If the box for ATD utilization is left blank, the ATD is not part of the approved course, and its use is not required.

Not checking the ATD box does not preclude a ground instructor from using an ATD. An ATD may be used in ground training just like any other classroom instructional aid.

THE FLIGHT TRAINING COURSE
The Flight Training Syllabus also is divided into three stages, each providing an important segment of pilot training. Each stage builds on previous learning and, therefore, should be completed in sequence. However, to provide some flexibility for adapting to individual student needs and the training environment, the syllabus lesson sequence may be altered with approval of the chief flight instructor. Any deviation should not disturb the course continuity or objectives.

STAGE I
In Stage I, the student develops the knowledge, skill, and habits necessary for safe solo flight. The basic maneuvers are introduced, practiced, and reviewed. In addition, the student practices airport operations, normal and crosswind takeoffs and landings, emergency procedures, and ground reference maneuvers.

NOTE: The student must complete the Presolo Exam and Briefing prior to the first solo flight, regardless of whether that flight occurs at the end of Stage I or at the beginning of Stage II. Guidance on administering the Presolo Exam is provided by AC 61-101, Presolo Written Test, and additional information is included in the Instructor's Guide chapter containing the pilot briefings.

Instructors also should review pertinent sections of Part 61. FAR 61.87(d) contains specific maneuvers and procedures required for presolo training. Although the terminology for some of these maneuvers and procedures differs somewhat between Part 141 and the ACS, it is important to ensure compliance with all presolo training requirements specified in Part 61.

STAGE II

This stage introduces short- and soft-field takeoffs, climbs, approaches, and landings; VOR, GPS, and ADF navigation (based on aircraft equipment); and night flying. The maneuvers introduced during this stage incorporate the skills developed during Stage I, and provide important skills necessary for the cross-country operations later in this stage.

The cross-country portion of this stage provides the information, knowledge, and skills that enable the student to begin cross-country operations. With the knowledge acquired during Stage II, the student should be able to safely conduct solo cross-country flights. Proficiency in advanced maneuvers and cross-country procedures will be evaluated during the stage check in Flight Lesson 20.

STAGE III

The flights of Stage III are designed to provide the student with the proficiency required for the private pilot practical test. These flights are devoted to gaining experience and confidence in cross-country operations and reviewing all maneuvers within the syllabus to attain maximum pilot proficiency. Student proficiency and knowledge will be assessed by the chief instructor, assistant chief instructor, or check instructor during the stage check in Flight Lesson 25. The student can pursue further review and instruction as necessary, in preparation for the End-of-Course Flight Check.

PREFLIGHT DISCUSSION

Prior to each dual and solo flight, the instructor should provide the student with thorough briefing of the tasks to be covered during the lesson. Select a quiet, private place to brief the student and explain the lesson content. The instructor should define unfamiliar terms, explain the maneuvers and objectives of each lesson, and discuss SRM concepts related to each lesson. The Preflight Discussion should be tailored to the specific flight, the local environment, and especially to the needs of the student.

FLIGHT SIMULATION TRAINING DEVICE (FSTD)

If the flight school uses a flight simulator or flight training device (FTD) in the private pilot training program, the syllabus allows for instruction in simulator or FTD sessions. Training in a simulator that meets the requirements of 141.41(a) may be credited for a maximum of 20 percent of the total flight training time requirements (20% × 35 hours = 7.0 hours). Training in an FTD that meets the requirements of 141.41(b) may be credited for a maximum of 15 percent of the total flight training hour requirements (15% × 35 hours = 5.25 hours).

AIRPLANE PRACTICE

An effective preflight discussion helps the student obtain the maximum benefit from each flight. Each flight should begin with a review of previously-learned maneuvers before any new maneuvers are introduced. To ensure that students efficiently utilize solo flight training lessons, the instructor should instruct the student in the maneuvers to be performed during the flight and what is expected to be accomplished during that lesson.

POSTFLIGHT DEBRIEFING

The Postflight Debriefing is as important as the Preflight Discussion. The student should perform a self-critique of maneuvers/procedures and single-pilot resource management (SRM). This *learner-centered grading* is especially helpful in developing decision-making skills. If a student is having trouble mastering a skill, make a plan for improving the performance of that skill. An effective postflight briefing increases retention and helps the student prepare for the next lesson.

As a guide, a minimum of 1/2 hour per flight is recommended for preflight and postflight briefings combined. This is the time an instructor could expect to spend with a well-prepared student. Some lessons will require additional time.

STUDENT STAGE CHECKS

Stage checks measure the student's accomplishments during each stage of training. The conduct of each stage check is the responsibility of the chief instructor. However, the chief instructor may delegate authority for conducting stage checks and the End-of-Course Flight Check to the assistant chief instructor or a designated check instructor. This procedure provides close supervision of training and provides another opinion on the student's progress. The stage check also helps the chief instructor check the effectiveness of the instructors.

An examination of the building-block theory of learning will show that it is extremely important for progress and proficiency to be satisfactory before the student enters a new stage of training. Therefore, the next stage should not begin until the student successfully completes the stage check. Failure to follow this progression may defeat the purpose of the stage check and degrade the overall effectiveness of the course.

PILOT BRIEFINGS

The following three pilot briefings are assigned in the flight syllabus.
1. Presolo Exam and Briefing
2. Solo Cross-Country Briefing
3. Private Pilot Practical Test Briefing

The pilot briefings material are located in the Instructor's Guide. Each briefing consists of a series of questions that cover the pertinent information. Instructors may provide students with the questions in advance of the actual briefing, so they can research the questions and gain optimum benefit from the briefing.

Conduct the briefings as private tutoring sessions to test each student's comprehension. Hold the briefings in a comfortable classroom or office environment, and schedule ample time. Discuss every question thoroughly to ensure students understand the key points. Complete the briefings during the Preflight Discussion for the appropriate flight. Correct placement of the briefings is indicated in the Lesson Time Allocation Table.

The Presolo Exam and Briefing is unique. As specified in FAR 61.87, the student must demonstrate satisfactory knowledge of the required subject areas by completing a knowledge exam. This exam is to be administered and graded by the instructor who endorses the student pilot certificate for solo flight and must

INTRODUCTION ■ **Private Pilot Course**

include questions on applicable portions of FAR Parts 61 and 91. In addition, instructors should modify the exam as necessary to make it appropriate for the aircraft to be flown and the local flying environment.

PART 61 OPERATION

The *Private Pilot Syllabus* is designed to meet all the requirements of Part 141, Appendix B. It can be adapted to meet the aeronautical knowledge, proficiency, and experience (airplane, single-engine) requirements of Part 61. (See FAR 61.105, 61.107, and 61.109). The basic difference between the flight time requirements of Part 141 and Part 61 is that under Part 61, the student must have at least 40 hours of flight time that includes at least 20 hours of flight instruction from an authorized instructor and 10 hours of solo flight training (in specified areas of operation). The flight time requirements of Part 141 are nearly the same, except total flight time is only 35 hours. Adapting this syllabus to Part 61 training requires only a slight modification of individual flight lesson times.

The ground training requirements under Part 61 specify that an applicant for a knowledge test must have a logbook endorsement from an authorized instructor who conducted the training or reviewed the applicant's home study course. The endorsement must indicate satisfactory completion of the ground instruction or home study course required for the certificate or rating being sought. A home study course for the purposes of Part 61 is a course of study in those aeronautical knowledge areas specified in FAR 61.105, and organized by a pilot school, publisher, flight or ground instructor, or by the student. The Jeppesen Private Pilot Course satisfies this requirement. As a practical consideration, students seeking pilot certification under Part 61 should receive some formal ground training, either in the classroom or from an authorized flight or ground instructor.

CREDIT FOR PREVIOUS TRAINING

According to FAR 141.77, when a student transfers from one FAA-approved school to another approved school, course credits obtained in the previous course of training may be credited for 50 percent of the curriculum requirements by the receiving school. However, the receiving school must determine the amount of credit to be allowed based upon a proficiency test or knowledge test, or both, conducted by the receiving school. A student who enrolls in a course of training may receive credit for 25 percent of the curriculum requirements for knowledge and experience gained in a non-Part 141 flight school, and the credit must be based upon a proficiency test or knowledge test, or both, conducted by the receiving school. The amount of credit for previous training allowed, whether received from an FAA-approved school or other source, is determined by the receiving school. In addition, the previous provider of the training must certify the kind and amount of training given, and the result of each stage check and end-of-course test, if applicable.

Course Overview

The Private Pilot Course is designed to coordinate the academic study assignments and flight training required to operate in an increasingly complex aviation environment. New subject matter is introduced and evaluated during the ground lessons using the following methods, as chosen by your school.

1. In-depth textbook assignments with study questions:
   ◊ *Private Pilot* Textbook/eBook
   ◊ *Private Pilot Maneuvers* Manual/eBook
2. The *Private Pilot online* course in the Jeppesen Online Learning Center
3. The *Private Pilot* video series on DVD
4. Instructor/student discussions
5. Stage exams and end-of-course exams

For best results, students should complete ground lessons just prior to the respective flight lessons, as outlined in the syllabus. However, it is also acceptable to present lessons in a formal ground school before introducing the student to the airplane. If a lot of time has elapsed between the ground lesson and the associated flight, the instructor should conduct a short review of essential material. Generally, flight lessons should not be conducted until the student has completed the prerequisite ground lessons.

In selected flight lessons, the abbreviation "VR" indicates that students should maintain aircraft control by using visual reference. "IR" indicates that they should use instrument references. No reference to either "VR" or "IR," indicates normal private pilot maneuvers or procedures by visual references.

THE PRIVATE PILOT CERTIFICATION COURSE AIRPLANE SINGLE-ENGINE LAND

COURSE OBJECTIVES
The student will obtain the knowledge, skill, and aeronautical experience necessary to meet the requirements for a private pilot certificate with an airplane category rating and a single-engine land class rating.

COURSE COMPLETION STANDARDS
The student must demonstrate through knowledge exams and flight checks, and show through appropriate records that he/she meets the knowledge, skill, and experience requirements necessary to obtain a private pilot certificate with an airplane category rating and a single-engine land class rating.

OVERVIEW ■ **Private Pilot Course**

STUDENT INFORMATION

COURSE ENROLLMENT
There are no prerequisites for initial enrollment in the ground portion of the Private Pilot course.

REQUIREMENTS FOR SOLO FLIGHT
Before you may fly solo, you must hold a recreational, sport, or student pilot certificate and at least a current third-class medical certificate. You must be at least 16 years of age to obtain a student pilot certificate and be able to read, speak, write, and understand the English language. Remember that solo flight operations require specific training, successful completion of a presolo knowledge exam, and endorsements from your flight instructor.

REQUIREMENTS FOR GRADUATION
To graduate, you must be at least 17 years of age, be able to read, speak, write, and understand the English language, meet the time requirements listed in the Lesson Time Allocation Table, and satisfactorily complete the training outlined in this syllabus. When you meet the minimum requirements of Part 141, Appendix B, you are eligible for graduation.

LESSON DESCRIPTION AND STAGES OF TRAINING
This syllabus describes each lesson, including the objectives, references, topics, and completion standards. The stage objectives and standards are described at the beginning of each stage within the syllabus.

FLIGHT CHECKS AND GROUND EXAMS
The syllabus incorporates stage checks and an end-of-course flight checks as required by Part 141, Appendix B. The chief instructor is responsible for ensuring that each student accomplishes the required stage checks and the End-of-Course Flight Check in accordance with the school's approved training course. However, the chief instructor may delegate authority for stage checks and the End-of-Course Flight Check to the assistant chief or check instructor. You also must complete the academic knowledge tests—stage exams, pilot briefings, and end-of-course final exams—that are described within the syllabus.

OVERVIEW ■ Private Pilot Course

Ground Training Overview

Completion of this course is based solely upon compliance with the minimum requirements of FAR Part 141. The accompanying tables with times shown in hours are provided mainly for guidance in achieving regulatory compliance.

PRIVATE PILOT CERTIFICATION COURSE
AIRPLANE SINGLE-ENGINE LAND

GROUND TRAINING						
	Maneuvers Class Discussion and Online Training	ATD	Ground Lessons	Pilot Briefings	Stage/ Final Exams	Exam Debriefings
GROUND STAGE I	3.0	3.0	10.0		1.0	As Required
GROUND STAGE II	3.0		6.0	2.0	1.0	As Required
GROUND STAGE III	3.0	2.0	8.0	2.0	4.0	1.0
TOTALS	9.0	5.0	24.0	4.0	6.0	1.0

NOTE: 1. The first column shows the recommended *Private Pilot Maneuvers* discussion, and/or online training time.
2. The second column shows maximum ATD time when an ATD is approved for the course.
3. The third column shows the minimum recommended training time for ground lessons, which may include class discussion, video presentations, or online lessons. Times shown in columns 1 and 2 may be credited toward the total time shown in column 3 as follows:
   • Up to 9 hours of *Private Pilot Maneuvers* class discussion, and online training.
   • Up to 5 hours of ATD training.
To recieve credit for ATD training time, the associated course approval must be obtained. (See Preface.)

Flight Training Overview

PRIVATE PILOT CERTIFICATION COURSE
AIRPLANE SINGLE-ENGINE LAND

	FLIGHT TRAINING							
	DUAL					**SOLO**		
	Day Local	Day Cross Country	Night Local	Night Cross Country	Instrument	Day Local	Cross Country	Dual/Solo Combined Totals
FLIGHT STAGE I	9.0 (8.5)				(1.0)	.5 (0)		9.5 (8.5)
FLIGHT STAGE II	4.0 (4.5)	2.0	1.0	2.0	(2.0)	2.0 (2.5)	2.5	13.5 (14.5)
FLIGHT STAGE III	6.0						6.0	12.0
TOTALS	19.0	2.0	1.0	2.0	(3.0)	2.5	8.5	35.0

NOTE: 1. The Presolo Written Exam, Briefing, and Flight Lesson 9 can be moved to Flight Stage II if the Stage Check precedes the first solo. The numbers in parentheses indicate the stage times if the Stage I Check precedes the first solo.

2. Dual instrument training in the airplane is allocated to portions of flight lessons 3, 4, 5, 7, 8, 14, 15, 17, and 18 for a total of 3.0 hours. The minimum recommended times are .2 hours (12 minutes) each for Flight Lesson 3, 4, 5, 7, and 8 and .5 hours (30 minutes) each for Flight Lessons 14, 15, 17, and 18. The total of 3.0 hours of instrument training is specified in Part 141, Appendix B.

3. For the purpose of meeting cross-country time requirements for a private pilot certificate, a landing must be accomplished at a straight-line distance of more than 50 nautical miles from the original point of departure.

Allocation Tables

LESSON TIME ALLOCATION

Maneuvers Class Discussion and Online Training	ATD	Ground Lessons	Pilot Briefings	Stage/Final Exams	Exam Debriefings		Day Local	Day Cross-Country	Night Local	Night Cross-Country	Instrument	Day Local	Cross-Country
Ground Training							**Flight Training**					**Solo**	
							Dual						
GROUND STAGE I, II AND FLIGHT STAGE I													
	1.0	2.0				Ground Lesson 1 – Discovering Aviation							
	1.0	2.0				Ground Lesson 2 – Airplane Systems							
						Flight Lesson 1	.5						
		2.0				Ground Lesson 3 – Aerodynamic Principles							
1.0						Flight Lesson 2	1.0						
		2.0				Ground Lesson 4 – The Flight Environment							
1.0						Flight Lesson 3	1.0				(.2)		
	1.0	2.0				Ground Lesson 5 – Communication & Flight Info.							
1.0						Flight Lesson 4	1.0				(.2)		
				1.0	As Req.	Ground Lesson 6 – Stage I Exam							
1.0						Flight Lesson 5	1.0				(.2)		
		2.0				Ground Lesson 7 – Meteorology for Pilots							
1.0						Flight Lesson 6	1.0						
		2.0				Ground Lesson 8 – Federal Aviation Regulations							
1.0						Flight Lesson 7	1.0				(.2)		
		2.0				Ground Lesson 9 – Interpreting Weather Data							
			2.0		As Req.	Presolo Exam and Briefing							
						Flight Lesson 8	1.0				(.2)		
						Flight Lesson 9 (First Solo)	.5					.5	
				1.0	As Req.	Ground Lesson 10 – Stage II Exam							
						Flight Lesson 10 – Stage Check	1.0						
6.0	3.0	16.0	2.0	2.0	As Req.	Ground Stage Totals	9.0 (8.5)				(1.0)	.5 (0)	

NOTE:
1. The first column shows the recommended *Private Pilot Maneuvers* discussion, and online training training time.
2. The second column shows maximum ATD time when an ATD is approved for the course.
3. The third column shows the minimum recommended training time for ground lessons, which may include class discussion, video presentations, or online lessons. Times shown in columns 1 and 2 may be credited toward the total time shown in column 3 for the Private Pilot Course as follows:
   - Up to 9 hours of *Private Pilot Maneuvers* class discussion and online training.
   - Up to 5 hours of ATD training.
   To recieve credit for ATD training time, the associated course approval must be obtained. (See Preface.)
4. The numbers in parentheses for Dual and Solo Day Local flight times represent total stage times if the Stage 1 check precedes the first solo.

OVERVIEW ■ Private Pilot Course

LESSON TIME ALLOCATION

Maneuvers Class Discussion and Online Training	ATD	Ground Lessons	Pilot Briefings	Stage/Final Exams	Exam Debriefings		Day Local	Day Cross-Country	Night Local	Night Cross-Country	Instrument	Day Local	Cross-Country
Ground Training							Flight Training — Dual					Solo	
	2.0					Ground Lesson 11 – Airplane Performance							
1.0						Flight Lesson 11	1.0						
	1.0	2.0				Ground Lesson 12 – Navigation							
						Flight Lesson 12						1.0	
		2.0				Ground Lesson 13 – Human Factor Principles							
						Flight Lesson 13						1.0	
	1.0	2.0				Ground Lesson 14 – Flying Cross Country							
1.0						Flight Lesson 14	1.0				(.5)		
				1.0	As Req.	Ground Lesson 15 – Stage III Exam							
						Flight Lesson 15	1.0				(.5)		
						Flight Lesson 16			1.0				
1.0						Flight Lesson 17		2.0			(.5)		
						Flight Lesson 18				2.0	(.5)		
			2.0			Briefing – Solo Cross-Country							
						Flight Lesson 19							2.5
				3.0	1.0	Ground Lesson 16 & 17 – Final Exams A & B							
						Flight Lesson 20 – Stage Check	1.0						
3.0	2.0	8.0	2.0	4.0	1.0	**Stage Totals**	4.0 (4.5)	2.0	1.0	2.0	(2.0)	2.0 (2.5)	2.5

GROUND STAGE III AND FLIGHT STAGE II

NOTE:
1. The first column shows the recommended *Private Pilot Maneuvers* discussion, and online training time.
2. The second column shows maximum ATD time when an ATD is approved for the course.
3. The third column shows the minimum recommended training time for ground lessons, which may include class discussion, video presentations, or online lessons. Times shown in columns 1 and 2 may be credited toward the total time shown in column 3 for the Private Pilot Course as follows:
   • Up to 9 hours of *Private Pilot Maneuvers* class discussion and online training.
   • Up to 5 hours of ATD training.
   To recieve credit for ATD training time, the associated course approval must be obtained. (See Preface.)
4. The numbers in parentheses for Dual and Solo Day Local flight times represent total stage times if the Stage 1 check precedes the first solo.

Private Pilot Syllabus

LESSON TIME ALLOCATION

Maneuvers Class Discussion and Online Training	ATD	Ground Lessons	Pilot Briefings	Stage/Final Exams	Exam Debriefings		Day Local	Day Cross-Country	Night Local	Night Cross-Country	Instrument	Day Local	Cross-Country
						Ground Training / **Flight Training** — Dual / Solo							
						FLIGHT STAGE III							
						Flight Lesson 21							2.0
						Flight Lesson 22							4.0
						Flight Lesson 23	2.0				As Req.		
						Flight Lesson 24	2.0				As Req.		
						Flight Lesson 25 – Stage Check	1.0						
			As Req.			Briefing – Private Pilot Practical Test							
						Flight Lesson 26 – End-of-Course Flight Check	1.0				As Req.		
						Stage Totals	6.0						6.0
9.0	5.0	24.0	4.0	6.0	1.0	Private Pilot Course – Overall Totals	19.0	2.0	1.0	2.0	(3.0)	2.5	8.5

The individual times shown on the accompanying Lesson Time Allocation tables are for instructor/student guidance only; they are not mandatory for each ground lesson, flight lesson, or stage of training. At the conclusion of this course, the student must meet the minimum requirements of FAR Part 141, Appendix B, for each catagory in order to graduate. Preflight and postflight briefing times are not specified, but a minimum of .5 hours for each dual and solo flight is suggested. The times for Pilot Briefings, although assigned and completed along with selected flight lessons, are considered part of ground training.

OVERVIEW ■ **Private Pilot Course**

Private Pilot Ground Training Syllabus

GROUND TRAINING COURSE OBJECTIVES

The student will obtain the required aeronautical knowledge and meet the prerequisites in Part 61 for the FAA Private Pilot Airman Knowledge Test.

GROUND TRAINING COURSE COMPLETION STANDARDS

Through knowledge exams and records, the student must demonstrate the knowledge necessary to pass the FAA Private Pilot Airman Knowledge Test and show that the prerequisites specified in Part 61 have been met.

Stage I

STAGE OBJECTIVES

During this stage, the student is introduced to pilot training, aviation opportunities, and human factors in aviation, and will become familiar with airplane systems, aerodynamic principles, and the flight environment. The student also will obtain a basic knowledge of the safety of flight, airports, aeronautical charts, airspace, and air traffic control services, including the use of radar. In addition, the student will learn radio procedures and the common sources of flight information.

STAGE COMPLETION STANDARDS

This stage is complete when the student passes the Stage I Exam with a minimum score of 80%, and the instructor has reviewed with the student each incorrect response to ensure complete understanding before starting Stage II.

GROUND LESSON 1

REFERENCES

NOTE: Students should study the listed references prior to beginning the Ground Lesson 1 instructional session.

Private Pilot Textbook/EBook
Chapter 1 — Discovering Aviation (Sections A, B, C)

Private Pilot Online — Jeppesen Learning Center
Module 1 — Discovering Aviation (GL 1, 2, 3)

OBJECTIVES

- Become familiar with pilot training, aviation opportunities, and human factors in aviation.
- Understand the essential components of the school's pilot training program.

CONTENT

COURSE OVERVIEW
- ❏ Course Elements and Materials
- ❏ Exams and Tests
- ❏ Policies and Procedures
- ❏ Student/Instructor Expectations
- ❏ Use of Flight Training Devices (FTDs) and Aviation Training Devices (ATDs)

SECTION A — PILOT TRAINING
GL 2 ONLINE — PILOT TRAINING FAQS
- ❏ How to Get Started
- ❏ Role of the FAA
- ❏ Fixed-Base Operators (FBOs)
- ❏ Eligibility Requirements
- ❏ Types of Training Available
- ❏ Phases of Training
- ❏ Private Pilot Privileges and Limitations

SECTION B — AVIATION OPPORTUNITIES
GL 1 ONLINE — AVIATION OPPORTUNITIES
- ❏ New Experiences
- ❏ Aviation Organizations
- ❏ Category/Class Ratings
- ❏ Additional Pilot Certificates
- ❏ Aviation Careers

SECTION C — INTRODUCTION TO HUMAN FACTORS
GL 3 ONLINE — INTRODUCTION TO HUMAN FACTORS
- ❏ Single-Pilot Resource Management
  - ◊ Aeronautical Decision Making
  - ◊ Risk Management
  - ◊ Task Management
  - ◊ Situational Awareness
  - ◊ CFIT Awareness
  - ◊ Automation Management
- ❏ Aviation Physiology
  - ◊ Alcohol, Drugs, and Performance
  - ◊ Fitness for Flight

STAGE I ■ Ground Training Syllabus

COMPLETION STANDARDS:

- Demonstrate understanding of pilot training programs, opportunities in aviation, and human factors during oral quizzing by the instructor.
- Demonstrate understanding of policies and procedures that apply to the school's pilot training program.
- If using the Private Pilot online course, complete the online exams for GL 2 and 3 with a minimum score of 80 percent. Review with the instructor each incorrect response to ensure complete understanding before starting Ground Lesson 2.

STUDY ASSIGNMENT

Private Pilot Textbook/EBook
Chapter 2 — Airplane Systems (Sections A, B, C)

Private Pilot Online — Jeppesen Learning Center
Module 2 — Airplane Systems (GL 4, 5, 6)

GROUND LESSON 2

REFERENCES

Private Pilot Textbook/EBook
Chapter 2 — Airplane Systems (Sections A, B, C)

Private Pilot Online — Jeppesen Learning Center
Module 2 — Airplane Systems (GL 4, 5, 6)

OBJECTIVES

- Gain a basic understanding of the main airplane components and systems.
- Learn about the powerplant and related systems.
- Become familiar with flight instrument functions and operating characteristics, including errors and common malfunctions.

CONTENT

SECTION A — AIRPLANES
GL 4 ONLINE — AIRPLANES
- ❏ Fuselage
- ❏ Wings
- ❏ Empennage
- ❏ Landing Gear
- ❏ Engine/Propeller
- ❏ Pilot's Operating Handbook (POH)

SECTION B — THE POWERPLANT AND RELATED SYSTEMS
GL 5 ONLINE — THE POWERPLANT AND RELATED SYSTEMS
❑ Reciprocating Engine
❑ Induction Systems
❑ Supercharging and Turbocharging
❑ Ignition Systems
❑ Fuel Systems
❑ Refueling
❑ Oil Systems
❑ Cooling Systems
❑ Exhaust Systems
❑ Propellers
❑ Propeller Hazards
❑ Electrical Systems

SECTION C — FLIGHT INSTRUMENTS
GL 6 ONLINE — FLIGHT INSTRUMENTS
❑ Pitot-Static Instruments
❑ Airspeed Indicator
❑ Altimeter
❑ Vertical Speed Indicator
❑ Gyroscopic Instruments
❑ Magnetic Compass

COMPLETION STANDARDS
• Demonstrate understanding of airplane components and systems, powerplant and related systems, and flight instruments during oral quizzing by the instructor.
• Complete with a minimum score of 80 percent: questions for Chapter 2A, 2B, and 2C, or online exams for GL 4, 5, and 6. Review with the instructor each incorrect response to ensure complete understanding before starting Ground Lesson 3.

STUDY ASSIGNMENT
Private Pilot Textbook/EBook
Chapter 3 — Aerodynamic Principles (Sections A, B, C)

Private Pilot Online — Jeppesen Learning Center
Module 3 — Aerodynamic Principles (GL 7, 8, 9)

GROUND LESSON 3

REFERENCES

Private Pilot Textbook/EBook
Chapter 3 — Aerodynamic Principles (Sections A, B, C)

Private Pilot Online — Jeppesen Learning Center
Module 3 — Aerodynamic Principles (GL 7, 8, 9)

OBJECTIVES
- Become familiar with aerodynamic principles, including the four forces of flight, stability, maneuvering flight, and load factor.
- Understand stall and spin characteristics as they relate to training airplanes.
- Learn the importance of prompt recognition of stalls.

CONTENT

SECTION A — FOUR FORCES OF FLIGHT
GL 7 ONLINE — FOUR FORCES OF FLIGHT
- ❏ Lift
- ❏ Airfoils
- ❏ Pilot Control of Lift
- ❏ Weight
- ❏ Thrust
- ❏ Drag
- ❏ Ground Effect

SECTION B — STABILITY
GL 8 ONLINE — STABILITY
- ❏ Three Axes of Flight
- ❏ Longitudinal Stability
- ❏ Center of Gravity Position
- ❏ Lateral Stability
- ❏ Directional Stability
- ❏ Stalls
- ❏ Spins

SECTION C — AERODYNAMICS OF MANEUVERING FLIGHT
GL 9 ONLINE — AERODYNAMICS OF MANEUVERING FLIGHT
- ❏ Climbing Flight
- ❏ Left-Turning Tendencies
- ❏ Descending Flight
- ❏ Turning Flight
- ❏ Load Factor

STAGE I ■ **Ground Training Syllabus**

COMPLETION STANDARDS
- Demonstrate understanding of stalls, spins, and basic aerodynamic principles during oral quizzing by the instructor.
- Complete with a minimum score of 80 percent: questions for Chapter 3A, 3B, and 3C; or online exams for GL 7, 8, and 9. Review with the instructor each incorrect response to ensure complete understanding before starting Ground Lesson 4.

STUDY ASSIGNMENT
Private Pilot Textbook/EBook
Chapter 4 — The Flight Environment (Sections A, B, C, D)

Private Pilot Online — Jeppesen Learning Center
Module 4 — The Flight Environment (GL 10, 11, 12, 13)

GROUND LESSON 4

REFERENCES

Private Pilot Textbook/EBook
Chapter 4 — The Flight Environment (Sections A, B, C, D)

Private Pilot Online — Jeppesen Learning Center
Module 4 — The Flight Environment (GL 10, 11, 12, 13)

OBJECTIVES
- Understand important safety considerations, including collision avoidance procedures, right-of-way rules, and minimum safe altitudes.
- Become familiar with airport marking and lighting, aeronautical charts, and types of airspace.
- Learn about collision avoidance procedures and runway incursion avoidance.

CONTENT

SECTION A — SAFETY OF FLIGHT
GL 10 ONLINE — SAFETY OF FLIGHT
- ❏ Collision Avoidance/Visual Scanning
- ❏ Airport Operations
- ❏ Right-of-Way Rules
- ❏ Minimum Safe Altitudes
- ❏ Taxiing in Wind
- ❏ Positive Exchange of Flight Controls

SECTION B — AIRPORTS
GL 11 ONLINE — AIRPORTS
- ❏ Controlled and Uncontrolled
- ❏ Runway Layout
- ❏ Traffic Pattern
- ❏ Airport Visual Aids
- ❏ Runway and Taxiway Markings
- ❏ Ramp Area Hand Signals
- ❏ Runway Incursion Avoidance
- ❏ Land and Hold Short Operations (LAHSO)
- ❏ Airport Lighting
- ❏ Visual Glide Path Indicators
- ❏ Approach Light Systems
- ❏ Pilot-Controlled Lighting

SECTION C — AERONAUTICAL CHARTS
GL 12 ONLINE — AERONAUTICAL CHARTS
- ❏ Latitude and Longitude
- ❏ Projections
- ❏ Sectional Aeronautical Charts
- ❏ Terminal Area Charts
- ❏ World Aeronautical Charts
- ❏ Chart Symbology

SECTION D — AIRSPACE
GL 13 ONLINE — AIRSPACE
- ❏ Classifications
- ❏ Uncontrolled Airspace
- ❏ Controlled Airspace
  - ◊ Class E
  - ◊ Class D
  - ◊ Class C
  - ◊ Class B
  - ◊ Class A
- ❏ Special VFR
- ❏ Special Use Airspace
- ❏ Other Airspace Areas
- ❏ Emergency Air Traffic Rules
- ❏ Air Defense Identification Zones
- ❏ Security-Related Flight Restrictions
- ❏ Intercept Procedures

STAGE I ■ **Ground Training Syllabus**

COMPLETION STANDARDS

- Demonstrate understanding of airport marking and lighting, runway incursion avoidance, collision avoidance, right-of-way rules, minimum safe altitudes, aeronautical charts, and airspace during oral quizzing by the instructor.
- Complete with a minimum score of 80 percent: questions for Chapter 4A, 4B, 4C, and 4D, or online exams for GL 10, 11, 12, and 13. Review with the instructor each incorrect response to ensure complete understanding before starting Ground Lesson 5.

STUDY ASSIGNMENT

Private Pilot Textbook/EBook
  Chapter 5 — Communication and Flight Information (Sections A, B, C)

Private Pilot Online — Jeppesen Learning Center
  Module 5 — Communication and Flight Information (GL 14, 15, 16)

GROUND LESSON 5

REFERENCES

Private Pilot Textbook/EBook
  Chapter 5 — Communication and Flight Information (Sections A, B, C)

Private Pilot Online — Jeppesen Learning Center
  Module 5 — Communication and Flight Information (GL 14, 15, 16)

OBJECTIVES

- Become familiar with radar, transponder operations, and FAA radar equipment and services for VFR aircraft.
- Understand the types of services provided by Flight Service.
- Learn how to use the radio for communication.
- Gain a basic understanding of the sources of flight information, particularly the *Aeronautical Information Manual* and FAA advisory circulars.

CONTENT

SECTION A — RADAR AND ATC SERVICES
GL 14 ONLINE — RADAR AND ATC SERVICES
- ❏ Radar
- ❏ Transponder Operation
- ❏ FAA Radar Systems
- ❏ VFR Radar Services
- ❏ Automatic Terminal Information Service (ATIS)
- ❏ Flight Service

SECTION B — RADIO PROCEDURES
GL 15 ONLINE — RADIO PROCEDURES
❏ VHF Communication Equipment
❏ Using the Radio
❏ Phonetic Alphabet
❏ Coordinated Universal Time
❏ Common Traffic Advisory Frequency (CTAF)
❏ ATC Facilities at Controlled Airports
❏ Lost Communication Procedures
❏ Emergency Procedures
❏ Emergency Locator Transmitters (ELTs)

SECTION C — SOURCES OF FLIGHT INFORMATION
GL 16 ONLINE — SOURCES OF FLIGHT INFORMATION
❏ *Airport/Facility Directory*
❏ Federal Aviation Regulations
❏ *Aeronautical Information Manual* (AIM)
❏ Notices to Airmen (NOTAMs)
❏ Advisory Circulars
❏ Jeppesen Information Services

COMPLETION STANDARDS
- Demonstrate understanding of radar and ATC services, radio procedures and sources of flight information during oral quizzing by the instructor.
- Complete with a minimum score of 80 percent: questions for Chapter 5A, 5B, and 5C, or online exams for GL 14, 15, and 16. Review with the instructor each incorrect response to ensure complete understanding before taking the Stage I Exam in Ground Lesson 6.

STUDY ASSIGNMENT
Private Pilot Textbook/EBook
Review Chapters 2 – 5 in preparation for the Stage I Exam.

Private Pilot Online — Jeppesen Learning Center
Review Modules 1 – 5 (GL 2 – 16) in preparation for the Stage I Exam.

STAGE I ■ **Ground Training Syllabus**

GROUND LESSON 6 — STAGE I EXAM

REFERENCES

Private Pilot Textbook/EBook
Chapters 2 – 5

Private Pilot Online — Jeppesen Learning Center
Modules 1 – 5 (GL 2 – 16)

OBJECTIVE

Demonstrate knowledge of the subjects covered in Ground Lessons 1 – 5.

NOTE: Students are not tested on textbook Chapter 1 or GL 1 online content.

CONTENT

STAGE I EXAM

If using Private Pilot Online in the Jeppesen Learning Center, you will find the Stage I Exam in Module 6.

❑ Airplane Systems
❑ Aerodynamic Principles
❑ The Flight Environment
❑ Communication and Flight Information

COMPLETION STANDARDS

To complete the lesson and stage, pass the Stage I Exam with a minimum score of 80 percent. Review with the instructor each incorrect response to ensure complete understanding before starting Stage II.

STUDY ASSIGNMENT

Private Pilot Textbook/EBook

Chapter 6 — Meteorology for Pilots (Sections A, B, C)

Private Pilot Online — Jeppesen Learning Center

Module 7 — Meteorology for Pilots (GL 17, 18, 19)

Stage II

STAGE OBJECTIVES

During this stage, the student becomes familiar with weather theory, typical weather patterns, and aviation weather hazards. In addition to meteorological theory, the student will learn how to obtain and interpret various weather reports, forecasts, and graphic charts. Finally, the student will become thoroughly familiar with the FARs as they apply to private pilot operations.

STAGE COMPLETION STANDARDS

This stage is complete when the student passes the Stage II Exam with a minimum score of 80%, and the instructor has reviewed with the student each incorrect response to ensure complete understanding before starting Stage III.

GROUND LESSON 7

REFERENCES

Private Pilot Textbook/EBook
Chapter 6 — Meteorology for Pilots (Sections A, B, C)

Private Pilot Online — Jeppesen Learning Center
Module 7 — Meteorology for Pilots (GL 17, 18, 19)

OBJECTIVES

- Learn the causes of various weather conditions, frontal systems, and hazardous weather phenomena.
- Understand how to recognize critical weather situations from the ground and during flight, including hazards associated with thunderstorms.
- Become familiar with the recognition and avoidance of wind shear and wake turbulence.

CONTENT

SECTION A — BASIC WEATHER THEORY
GL 17 ONLINE — BASIC WEATHER THEORY
- ❑ The Atmosphere
- ❑ Atmospheric Circulation
- ❑ Atmospheric Pressure
- ❑ Coriolis Force
- ❑ Global Wind Patterns
- ❑ Local Wind Patterns

SECTION B — WEATHER PATTERNS
GL 18 ONLINE — WEATHER PATTERNS
- ❏ Atmospheric Stability
- ❏ Temperature Inversions
- ❏ Moisture
- ❏ Humidity
- ❏ Dewpoint
- ❏ Clouds and Fog
- ❏ Precipitation
- ❏ Airmasses
- ❏ Fronts

SECTION C — WEATHER HAZARDS
GL 19 ONLINE — WEATHER HAZARDS
- ❏ Thunderstorms
- ❏ Turbulence
- ❏ Wake Turbulence
- ❏ Wind Shear
- ❏ Microburst
- ❏ Icing
- ❏ Restrictions to Visibility
- ❏ Volcanic Ash

COMPLETION STANDARDS
- Demonstrate understanding of basic weather theory, weather patterns, and weather hazards during oral quizzing by the instructor.
- Complete with a minimum score of 80 percent: questions for Chapter 6A, 6B, and 6C, or online exams for GL 17, 18, and 19. Review incorrect responses with the instructor to ensure complete understanding before starting Ground Lesson 8.

STUDY ASSIGNMENT

FAR/AIM Manual/EBook
Private Pilot FARs

Private Pilot Online — Jeppesen Learning Center
Module 9 — Federal Aviation Regulations (FARs) (GL 23, 24)

GROUND LESSON 8

REFERENCES

FAR/AIM Manual/EBook
Private Pilot FARs

Private Pilot Online — Jeppesen Learning Center
Module 9 — Federal Aviation Regulations (FARs) (GL 23, 24)

OBJECTIVES

- Understand the appropriate Federal Aviation Regulations in the FAR Private Pilot Airplane Recommended Study List.
- Gain specific knowledge of those FARs which govern student solo flight operations, private pilot privileges and limitations, and National Transportation Safety Board (NTSB) accident reporting requirements.

CONTENT

- ❏ FAR Part 1
- ❏ FAR Part 61
- ❏ FAR Part 91
- ❏ NTSB 830

COMPLETION STANDARDS

- Demonstrate understanding of the relevant regulations in 14 CFR (FAR) Part 1, 61, 91, and 49 CFR (NTSB) 830 during oral quizzing by the instructor.
- If using the Private Pilot online course, complete the online exams for GL 23 and 24 with a minimum score of 80 percent. Review with the instructor each incorrect response to ensure complete understanding before starting Ground Lesson 9.

STUDY ASSIGNMENT

Private Pilot Textbook/EBook
Chapter 7 — Interpreting Weather Data (Sections A, B, C, D)

Private Pilot Online — Jeppesen Learning Center
Module 8 — Interpreting Weather Data (GL 20, 21, 22)

GROUND LESSON 9

REFERENCES

Private Pilot Textbook/EBook
Chapter 7 — Interpreting Weather Data (Sections A, B, C, D)

Private Pilot Online — Jeppesen Learning Center
Module 8 — Interpreting Weather Data (GL 20, 21, 22)

OBJECTIVES

- Learn how to obtain and interpret weather reports, formats, and graphic charts.
- Become familiar with the sources of weather information during preflight planning and while in flight.
- Recognize critical weather situations described by weather reports and forecasts.

STAGE II ■ **Ground Training Syllabus**

CONTENT

SECTION A — THE FORECASTING PROCESS
GL 20 ONLINE — PRINTED REPORTS AND FORECASTS
❏ Forecasting Methods
❏ Types of Forecasts
❏ Compiling and Processing Weather Data
❏ Forecasting Accuracy and Limitations

SECTION B — PRINTED REPORTS AND FORECASTS
GL 20 ONLINE — PRINTED REPORTS AND FORECASTS
❏ Aviation Routine Weather Report (METAR)
❏ Radar Weather Reports
❏ Pilot Weather Reports
❏ Terminal Aerodrome Forecast (TAF)
❏ Aviation Area Forecast
❏ Winds and Temperatures Aloft Forecast
❏ Severe Weather Reports and Forecasts
❏ AIRMET/SIGMET/Convective SIGMET

SECTION C — GRAPHIC WEATHER PRODUCTS
GL 21 — GRAPHIC WEATHER REPORTS AND FORECASTS
❏ Surface Analysis Chart
❏ Weather Depiction Chart
❏ Radar Summary Chart
❏ Satellite Weather Pictures
❏ Low-Level Significant Weather Prog
❏ Convective Outlook Chart
❏ Forecast Winds and Temperatures Aloft Chart
❏ Volcanic Ash Forecast and Dispersion Chart

SECTION D — SOURCES OF WEATHER INFORMATION
GL 22 ONLINE — SOURCES OF WEATHER INFORMATION
❏ Preflight Weather Sources
❏ In-Flight Weather Sources
❏ Enroute Flight Advisory Service
❏ Weather Radar Services
❏ Automated Weather Reporting Systems

COMPLETION STANDARDS
• Demonstrate understanding of material during oral quizzing by the instructor.
• Complete with a minimum score of 80 percent: questions for Chapter 2A, 2B, and 2C, or online exams for GL 4, 5, and 6. Review with the instructor each incorrect response to ensure complete understanding before taking the Stage II Exam in Ground Lesson 10.

STUDY ASSIGNMENT

Private Pilot and FAR/AIM Books/EBooks
Review Chapters 6 and 7, and the private pilot regulations in preparation for the Stage II Exam.

Private Pilot Online — Jeppesen Learning Center
Review Modules 7 – 9 (GL 17 – 24) in preparation for the Stage II Exam.

GROUND LESSON 10
STAGE II EXAM

REFERENCES

Private Pilot Textbook/EBook
Chapters 6 and 7

FAR/AIM Manual/EBook
Private Pilot FARs

Private Pilot Online — Jeppesen Learning Center
Modules 7 – 9 (GL 17 – 24)

OBJECTIVE
Demonstrate knowledge of the subjects covered in Ground Lessons 7 – 9.

CONTENT
If using Private Pilot Online in the Jeppesen Learning Center, you will find the Stage II Exam in Module 10.

STAGE II EXAM
❑ Meteorology for Pilots
❑ Federal Aviation Regulations
❑ Interpreting Weather Data

STUDY ASSIGNMENT

Private Pilot Textbook/EBook
Chapter 8 — Airplane Performance (Sections A, B, C)

Private Pilot Online — Jeppesen Learning Center
Module 11 — Airplane Performance (GL 25, 26, 27)

COMPLETION STANDARDS
This lesson and stage are complete when the student passes the Stage II Exam with a minimum score of 80%, and the instructor has reviewed with the student each incorrect response to ensure complete understanding before starting Stage III.

Stage III

STAGE III ■ Ground Training Syllabus

STAGE OBJECTIVES

During this stage, the student learns how to predict performance and control the weight and balance condition of the airplane. In addition, the student will be introduced to pilotage, dead reckoning, and navigation equipment. This includes understanding the basic concepts of how to use aeronautical charts, plotters, flight computers, and flight publications to plan cross-country flights. The student also will learn how to use VOR, ADF, and advanced navigation systems, including GPS. In addition, the student will obtain an understanding of the physiological factors that can affect both the pilot and passengers during flight. Finally, the student will learn how to conduct comprehensive preflight planning for cross-country flights and gain insight into factors affecting aeronautical decision making.

STAGE COMPLETION STANDARDS

This stage is complete when the student passes the Stage III Exam with a minimum score of 80%, and the instructor has reviewed with the student each incorrect response to ensure complete understanding before administering the End-of-Course Final Exams.

GROUND LESSON 11

REFERENCES

Private Pilot Textbook/EBook
Chapter 8 — Airplane Performance (Sections A, B, C)

Private Pilot Online — Jeppesen Learning Center
Module 11 — Airplane Performance (GL 25, 26, 27)

OBJECTIVES

- Learn how to use data supplied by the manufacturer to predict airplane performance, including takeoff and landing distances and fuel requirements.
- Learn to compute and control the weight and balance condition of a typical training airplane.
- Become familiar with basic functions of aviation computers.
- Understand the effects of density altitude on takeoff and climb performance.

Private Pilot Syllabus

CONTENT

SECTION A — PREDICTING PERFORMANCE
GL 26 ONLINE— PREDICTING PERFORMANCE
- ❏ Aircraft Performance and Design
- ❏ Chart Presentations
- ❏ Factors Affecting Performance
- ❏ Takeoff and Landing Performance
- ❏ Climb Performance
- ❏ Cruise Performance
- ❏ Using Performance Charts

SECTION B — WEIGHT AND BALANCE
GL 25 ONLINE — WEIGHT AND BALANCE
- ❏ Importance of Weight
- ❏ Importance of Balance
- ❏ Terminology
- ❏ Principles of Weight and Balance
- ❏ Weight and Balance Methods—Computation, Table, and Graph
- ❏ Weight-Shift Formula
- ❏ Effects of Operating at High Total Weights
- ❏ Flight at Various CG Positions

SECTION C — FLIGHT COMPUTERS
GL 27 ONLINE — MECHANICAL FLIGHT COMPUTERS
- ❏ Mechanical Flight Computers
- ❏ Time, Speed, and Distance
- ❏ Airspeed and Density Altitude Computations
- ❏ Wind Problems
- ❏ Conversions
- ❏ Multi-Part Problems

COMPLETION STANDARDS
- Calculate airplane performance and weight and balance using performance charts and a flight computer and discuss the results with the instructor.
- Complete with a minimum score of 80 percent: questions for Chapter 8A, 8B, and 8C, or online exams for GL 25, 26, and 27. Review with the instructor each incorrect response to ensure complete understanding before starting Ground Lesson 12.

STUDY ASSIGNMENT
Private Pilot Textbook/EBook
  Chapter 9 — Navigation (Sections A, B, C, D)

Private Pilot Online — Jeppesen Learning Center
  Module 12 — Navigation (GL 28, 29, 30, 31)

STAGE III ■ Ground Training Syllabus

GROUND LESSON 12

REFERENCES

Private Pilot Textbook/EBook
Chapter 9 — Navigation (Sections A, B, C, D)

Private Pilot Online — Jeppesen Learning Center
Module 12 — Navigation (GL 28, 29, 30, 31)

OBJECTIVES
- Learn the basic concepts of VFR flight planning, navigation using pilotage, dead reckoning, and aircraft navigation systems.
- Become familiar with the guidelines and recommended procedures related to flight planning, use of an FAA Flight Plan, VFR cruising altitudes, and lost procedures.
- Gain a basic understanding of VFR navigation using pilotage, dead reckoning, and navigation systems.

CONTENT

SECTION A — PILOTAGE AND DEAD RECKONING
GL 28 ONLINE — PILOTAGE AND DEAD RECKONING
❏ Pilotage
❏ Dead Reckoning
❏ Flight Planning
❏ VFR Cruising Altitudes
❏ Flight Plan
❏ Lost Procedures

SECTION B — VOR NAVIGATION
GL 29 ONLINE — VOR NAVIGATION
❏ Ground and Airborne Equipment
❏ VOR Orientation and Navigation
❏ VOR Checkpoints and Test Signals
❏ VOR Precautions
❏ Horizontal Situation Indicator
❏ Distance Measuring Equipment (DME)

SECTION C — ADF NAVIGATION
GL 31 ONLINE — ADF NAVIGATION
❏ ADF Equipment
❏ Orientation
❏ Homing
❏ ADF Intercepts and Tracking
❏ Movable-Card Indicator

❑ Radio Magnetic Indicator
❑ ADF Limitations

SECTION D — ADVANCED NAVIGATION
GL 30 ONLINE — GPS NAVIGATION
❑ Area Navigation
❑ Inertial Navigation System
❑ Global Positioning System (GPS)

COMPLETION STANDARDS
- Create a flight plan as assigned by the instructor and review the flight plan with the instructor.
- Demonstrate understanding of pilotage and dead reckoning, VOR navigation, ADF navigation, and GPS navigation during oral quizzing by the instructor.
- Complete with a minimum score of 80 percent: questions for Chapter 9A, 9B, 9C, and 9D, or online exams for GL 28, 29, 30, and 31. Review with the instructor each incorrect response to ensure complete understanding before starting Ground Lesson 13.

STUDY ASSIGNMENT

Private Pilot Textbook/EBook
Chapter 10 — Applying Human Factors Principles (Sections A, B)

Private Pilot Online — Jeppesen Learning Center
Module 13 — Applying Human Factors Principles (GL 32, 33)

GROUND LESSON 13

REFERENCES

Private Pilot Textbook/EBook
Chapter 10 — Applying Human Factors Principles (Sections A, B)

Private Pilot Online — Jeppesen Learning Center
Module 13 — Applying Human Factors Principles (GL 32, 33)

OBJECTIVES
- Gain insight into important aviation physiological factors as they relate to private pilot operations.
- Become familiar with single-pilot resource management (SRM) and understand its importance.
- Understand how to apply the aeronautical decision making process to make effective choices during flight operations.
- Become familiar with tools used to perform self-assessments, communicate effectively, manage tasks and resources, and to maintain situational awareness.

STAGE III ■ **Ground Training Syllabus**

STAGE III ■ Ground Training Syllabus

CONTENT

SECTION A — AVIATION PHYSIOLOGY
❏ Vision in Flight
❏ Night Vision
❏ Visual Illusions
❏ Disorientation
❏ Respiration
❏ Hypoxia
❏ Hyperventilation

SECTION B — SINGLE-PILOT RESOURCE MANAGEMENT (SRM)
❏ Aeronautical Decision Making (ADM)
  ◊ Applying the Decision Making Process
  ◊ Pilot-in-Command Responsibility
  ◊ Hazardous Attitudes
❏ Risk Management
❏ Task Management
❏ Situational Awareness
❏ CFIT Awareness
❏ Automation Management
❏ SRM Training

COMPLETION STANDARDS
• Demonstrate understanding of human factors principles, including SRM, during oral quizzing by the instructor.
• Complete with a minimum score of 80 percent: questions for Chapter 10A and 10B, or online exams for GL 32 and 33. Review with the instructor each incorrect response to ensure complete understanding before starting Ground Lesson 14.

STUDY ASSIGNMENT

Private Pilot Textbook/EBook
Chapter 11 — Flying Cross-Country (Sections A, B)

Private Pilot Online — Jeppesen Learning Center
Module 14 — Flying Cross Country (GL 34, 35)

GROUND LESSON 14

REFERENCES

Private Pilot Textbook/EBook
Chapter 11 — Flying Cross-Country (Sections A, B)

Private Pilot Online — Jeppesen Learning Center
Module 14 — Flying Cross Country (GL 34, 35)

OBJECTIVES
- Gain proficiency in planning a cross-country flight.
- Become familiar with the details of flying a typical cross-country flight, including locating checkpoints, making in-flight time and fuel calculations, and evaluating weather conditions.
- Understand how to make decisions regarding alternative actions, such as implementing a diversion.

CONTENT

SECTION A — THE FLIGHT PLANNING PROCESS
GL 34 ONLINE— THE FLIGHT PLANNING PROCESS
- ❏ Developing the Route
- ❏ Preflight Weather Briefing
- ❏ Completing the Navigation Log
- ❏ Flight Plan
- ❏ Preflight Inspection

SECTION B — THE FLIGHT
GL 35 ONLINE — THE FLIGHT
- ❏ Fundamentals of Flight Monitoring
- ❏ Departure
- ❏ Centennial Airport to Pueblo Memorial Airport
- ❏ Pueblo Memorial Airport to La Junta Municipal Airport
- ❏ La Junta Municipal Airport to Centennial Airport
- ❏ Diversion to Limon Municipal Airport
- ❏ Return to Centennial Airport

STUDY ASSIGNMENT

Private Pilot Textbook/EBook
Review Chapters 8 – 11 in preparation for the Stage III Exam

Private Pilot Online — Jeppesen Learning Center
Review Modules 11 – 14 in preparation for the Stage III Exam

COMPLETION STANDARDS
- Demonstrate understanding of the flight planning process and of using a flight plan during the flight during oral quizzing by the instructor.
- Complete with a minimum score of 80 percent: questions for Chapter 11A and 11B, or online exams for GL 34 and 35. Review with the instructor each incorrect response to ensure complete understanding before taking the Stage III Exam in Ground Lesson 15.

STAGE III ■ Ground Training Syllabus

GROUND LESSON 15
STAGE III EXAM

REFERENCES

Private Pilot Textbook/EBook
Chapters 8 – 11

Private Pilot Online — Jeppesen Learning Center
Modules 11 – 14 (GL 25 – 35)

OBJECTIVE
Demonstrate knowledge of the subjects covered in Ground Lessons 11 – 14.

CONTENT

STAGE III EXAM
❏ Airplane Performance
❏ Navigation
❏ Applying Human Factors Principles
❏ Flying Cross-Country

STUDY ASSIGNMENT

Private Pilot Textbook/EBook

Private Pilot Online — Jeppesen Learning Center

Review the entire textbook or online course, as necessary, in preparation for the End-of-Course Final Exam "A."

COMPLETION STANDARDS

This stage is complete when the student passes the Stage III Exam with a minimum score of 80%, and the instructor has reviewed with the student each incorrect response to ensure complete understanding before administering the End-of-Course Final Exams.

GROUND LESSON 16
END-OF-COURSE FINAL EXAM "A"

REFERENCES

Private Pilot Textbook/EBook
Chapters 1 – 11

Private Pilot Online — Jeppesen Learning Center
Modules 1 – 14 (GL 1 – 35)

OBJECTIVE
Demonstrate comprehension of the material presented in this course in preparation for the FAA Private Pilot Airman Knowledge Test.

CONTENT
❑ Private Pilot End-of-Course Final Exam "A"

STUDY ASSIGNMENT

Review any deficient subject areas based on the results of End-of-Course Final Exam "A." Review in preparation for End-of-Course Final Exam "B."

COMPLETION STANDARDS
Complete the End-of-Course Final Exam "A" with a minimum score of 80% and review with the instructor each incorrect response to ensure complete understanding before taking the End-of-Course Final Exam "B."

GROUND LESSON 17
END-OF-COURSE FINAL EXAM "B"

REFERENCES

Private Pilot Textbook/EBook
Chapters 1 – 11

Private Pilot Online — Jeppesen Learning Center
Modules 1 – 14 (GL 1 – 35)

STAGE III ■ **Ground Training Syllabus**

OBJECTIVES

Demonstrate comprehension of the academic material presented in this course and readiness to complete the FAA Private Pilot Airman Knowledge Test.

CONTENT

❑ Private Pilot End-of-Course Final Exam "B"

STUDY ASSIGNMENT

Review any deficient subject areas based on the results of End-of-Course Final Exam "B." Review in preparation for the FAA Private Pilot Airman Knowledge Test.

COMPLETION STANDARDS

Complete the End-of-Course Final Exam "B" with a minimum score of 80% and review with the instructor each incorrect response to ensure complete understanding so that the instructor can provide recommendation to take the Private Pilot Airman Knowledge Test.

STAGE III ■ **Ground Training Syllabus**

24

Private Pilot Flight Training Syllabus

FLIGHT TRAINING COURSE OBJECTIVES

The student will obtain the necessary aeronautical skill and experience necessary to meet the requirements for a private pilot certificate with an airplane category rating and single-engine land class rating.

FLIGHT TRAINING COURSE COMPLETION STANDARDS

The student must demonstrate through flight tests and school records that the necessary aeronautical skill and experience requirements to obtain a private pilot certificate with an airplane category rating and single-engine land class rating have been met.

Stage I

STAGE OBJECTIVES

During this stage, the student obtains the foundation for all future aviation training. The student becomes familiar with the training airplane and learns how the airplane controls are used to establish and maintain specific flight attitudes and ground tracks. The student also gains the proficiency to solo the training airplane in the traffic pattern.

STAGE COMPLETION STANDARDS

At the completion of this stage, the student will demonstrate proficiency in basic flight maneuvers, and will have successfully soloed in the traffic pattern (unless the Stage I Check precedes the first solo flight lesson, in which case, the first solo flight lesson moves to the beginning of Stage II). In addition, the student will gain the proficiency required for the introduction of maximum-performance takeoff and landing procedures in Stage II.

FLIGHT LESSON 1
DUAL — LOCAL (0.5)

NOTE: As indicated in the lesson time allocation tables, complete Ground Lessons 1 and 2 prior to this flight.

OBJECTIVES
- Become familiar with the training airplane and its systems.
- Identify the certificates and documents that are required to be in the airplane.
- Understand the use of checklists during the preflight inspection, engine starting, before-takeoff, after-landing, parking, and securing procedures.
- Understand how to taxi the airplane, including using the brakes.
- Learn how to use the flight controls to maintain specific attitudes.

PREFLIGHT DISCUSSION
❑ Fitness for Flight
❑ Medical Certificate Class and Duration
❑ Pilot Logbook or Flight Records
❑ Private Pilot Certificate Privileges, Limitations, and Recent Flight Experience Requirements
❑ Airworthiness Requirements
  ◊ Aircraft Logbooks
  ◊ Airplane Servicing
  ◊ Fuel Grades

INTRODUCE

PREFLIGHT PREPARATION
❑ Use of Checklists
❑ Preflight Inspection
❑ Airplane Certificates and Documents
❑ Airplane Servicing
  ◊ Fuel, Oil, Tires, and Struts
  ◊ Location of First Aid Kit
  ◊ Location of Fire Extinguisher

PREFLIGHT PROCEDURES
❑ Cockpit Management
❑ Operation of Systems
❑ Engine Starting
❑ Radio Communications
❑ Positive Exchange of Flight Controls
❑ Taxiing
❑ Runway Incursion Avoidance
❑ Before-Takeoff Check

TAKEOFFS, LANDINGS, AND GO-AROUNDS
❑ Normal Takeoff and Climb
❑ Normal Approach and Landing
❑ After Landing, Parking, and Securing

FUNDAMENTALS OF FLIGHT
❑ Collision Avoidance Procedures
❑ Use of Trim Control

- ❑ Straight-and-Level Flight
- ❑ Climbs, Descents, and Leveloffs
- ❑ Medium Banked Turns in Both Directions

COMPLETION STANDARDS

- Display basic knowledge of aircraft systems and the necessity of checking their operation before flight.
- Demonstrate familiarity with the control systems and how to use them to maneuver the airplane on the ground and in the air.

POSTFLIGHT DEBRIEFING

- ❑ Critique maneuvers/procedures and SRM.
- ❑ Update the record folder and logbook.

STUDY ASSIGNMENT

Ground Lesson 3
 Aerodynamic Principles

Private Pilot Maneuvers Manual/EBook
 Ground Operations and Basic Maneuvers

Maneuvers Lessons, Private Pilot Online — Jeppesen Learning Center
 ML01 — Straight-and-Level Flight
 ML02 — Climbs
 ML03 — Descents
 ML04 — Turns

FLIGHT LESSON 2
DUAL — LOCAL (1.0)

REFERENCES

Private Pilot Maneuvers Manual/EBook
 Ground Operations and Basic Maneuvers

Private Pilot Online — Jeppesen Learning Center
 Maneuvers 1, 2, 3, 4

STAGE I ■ **Flight Training Syllabus**

OBJECTIVES
- Gain proficiency in the procedures and maneuvers introduced in Flight Lesson 1, especially preflight activities, ground operations, and attitude control during basic maneuvers using visual reference (VR).
- Learn the elements of crosswind taxiing, turns, and flying at various airspeeds.
- Understand collision avoidance and runway incursion avoidance procedures.

PREFLIGHT DISCUSSION
❑ Human Factors Concepts
❑ Single Pilot Resource Management (SRM)
❑ Aeronautical Decision Making (ADM)
❑ Engine Starting
❑ Airport, Runway, and Taxiway Signs, Markings, and Lighting
❑ Crosswind Taxiing
❑ Collision Avoidance Procedures
❑ Airspeed and Configuration Changes

INTRODUCE
❑ Aviation Security
❑ Airport, Runway, and Taxiway Signs, Markings, and Lighting
❑ Crosswind Taxiing
❑ Turns to Headings
❑ Airspeed and Configuration Changes
❑ Flight at Approach Airspeed
❑ Traffic Patterns
❑ Descents in High and Low Drag Configurations

REVIEW
❑ Use of Checklists
❑ Preflight Inspection
❑ Certificates and Documents
❑ Airplane Servicing
❑ Cockpit Management
❑ Operation of Systems
❑ Engine Starting
❑ Radio Communications
❑ Positive Exchange of Flight Controls
❑ Runway Incursion Avoidance
❑ Before-Takeoff Check
❑ Normal Takeoff and Climb
❑ Collision Avoidance Procedures
❑ Straight-and-Level Flight
❑ Climbs, Descents, and Leveloffs
❑ Normal Approach and Landing
❑ After Landing, Parking, and Securing

COMPLETION STANDARDS

- Perform the preflight activities, ground operations, and coordinated airplane attitude control with instructor assistance.
- Perform taxiing and takeoffs with instructor assistance.
- Explain how to use the controls to maintain altitude within ± 250 feet during airspeed and configuration changes.
- Explain how to control attitude by visual reference (VR).

POSTFLIGHT DEBRIEFING

- ❏ Critique maneuvers/procedures and SRM.
- ❏ Create a plan for skills that need improvement.
- ❏ Update the record folder and logbook.

STUDY ASSIGNMENT

Ground Lesson 4
The Flight Environment

FLIGHT LESSON 3
DUAL — LOCAL (1.0)

NOTE: A view-limiting device is required for the 0.2 hours of dual instrument time allocated to Flight Lesson 3.

REFERENCES

Private Pilot Maneuvers Manual/EBook
Ground Operations and Basic Maneuvers

Private Pilot Online — Jeppesen Learning Center
Maneuvers 1, 2, 3, 4

OBJECTIVES

- Gain proficiency in controlling airspeed during basic maneuvers and traffic pattern operations.
- Become familiar with stalls from various flight attitudes in order to increase understanding of airplane control during normal and critical flight conditions.
- Begin controlling the airplane attitude by instrument reference (IR).
- Properly execute basic maneuvers and procedures, particularly takeoffs, traffic patterns, and landings.

PREFLIGHT DISCUSSION

- ❏ Single-Pilot Resource Management (SRM)
    - ◊ Task Management
    - ◊ Situational Awareness
- ❏ Positive Aircraft Control
- ❏ Basic Instrument Maneuvers

- ❏ Preflight Planning, Operation of Powerplant, Aircraft Systems, and Engine Runup Procedures
- ❏ Visual Scanning and Collision Avoidance Procedures
- ❏ Wind Shear and Wake Turbulence Avoidance Procedures

INTRODUCE
- ❏ Flight at Various Airspeeds From Cruise to Slow Flight
- ❏ Climbing And Descending Turns
- ❏ Maneuvering During Slow Flight
- ❏ Power-Off Stalls
- ❏ Power-On Stalls
- ❏ Straight-and-Level Flight (IR)
- ❏ Constant Airspeed Climbs (IR)
- ❏ Constant Airspeed Descents (IR)

REVIEW
- ❏ Use of Checklists
- ❏ Airplane Servicing
- ❏ Preflight Inspection
- ❏ Airworthiness Requirements
- ❏ Engine Starting
- ❏ Radio Communications
- ❏ Crosswind Taxi
- ❏ Before-Takeoff Check
- ❏ Normal Takeoff and Climb
- ❏ Traffic Patterns
- ❏ Collision Avoidance Procedures
- ❏ Turns to Headings
- ❏ Airspeed and Configuration Changes
- ❏ Descents in High and Low Drag Configurations
- ❏ Flight at Approach Airspeed
- ❏ Normal Approach and Landing
- ❏ Airport, Runway, and Taxiway Signs,
- ❏ Markings, and Lighting
- ❏ Parking and Securing the Airplane

COMPLETION STANDARDS
- Display increased proficiency in coordinated airplane attitude control during basic maneuvers.
- Perform unassisted takeoffs.
- Demonstrate correct communications and traffic pattern procedures.
- Complete landings with instructor assistance.
- Maintain altitude within ± 250 feet during airspeed transitions and while maneuvering at slow airspeeds.
- Display the basic ability to control attitude by instrument reference (IR).

POSTFLIGHT DEBRIEFING
❏ Critique maneuvers/procedures and SRM.
❏ Create a plan for skills that need improvement.
❏ Update the record folder and logbook.

STUDY ASSIGNMENT

Ground Lesson 5
Communication & Flight Information

Private Pilot Maneuvers Manual/EBook
Flight Maneuvers and Emergency Landing Procedures

Maneuvers Lessons, Private Pilot Online — Jeppesen Learning Center
ML05 — Slow Flight
ML06 — Stalls
ML07 — Steep Turns
ML08 — Attitude Instrument Flying
ML11 — Systems and Equipment Malfunctions
ML12 — Emergency Descent
ML13 — Emergency Approach and Landing

FLIGHT LESSON 4
DUAL — LOCAL (1.0)

NOTE: A view-limiting device is required for the 0.2 hours of dual instrument time allocated to Flight Lesson 4.

NOTE: All preflight duties and procedures will be performed and evaluated prior to each flight. Therefore, they will not appear in the content outlines.

REFERENCES

Private Pilot Maneuvers Manual/EBook
Flight Maneuvers
Emergency Landing Procedures

Private Pilot Online — Jeppesen Learning Center
Maneuvers Lessons 5, 6, 7, 8 — Flight Maneuvers
Maneuvers Lessons 11, 12, 13 — Emergency Procedures

OBJECTIVES
• Gain additional proficiency in controlling the airplane by instrument reference (IR) and in the maneuvers and procedures listed for review.
• Recognize and recover from stalls.
• Learn and practice the maneuvers and procedures listed for introduction, including emergency operations, and steep turns,
• Learn about secondary, accelerated maneuver, cross-control, and elevator trim stalls by observing instructor demonstration.

PREFLIGHT DISCUSSION
❑ Risk Management
❑ Pilot-in-Command Responsibility
❑ Systems and Equipment Malfunctions
❑ Emergency Field Selection

INTRODUCE
❑ Systems and Equipment Malfunctions
❑ Emergency Descent
❑ Emergency Approach and Landing (Simulated)
❑ Emergency Equipment and Survival Gear
❑ Climbing and Descending Turns (IR)
❑ Steep Turns
❑ Turns to Headings (IR)
❑ Flight at Slow Airspeeds with Realistic Distractions, and the Recognition and Recovery from Stalls Entered from Straight Flight and from Turns
❑ Stall/Spin Awareness
❑ Demonstrated Stalls
  (Secondary, Accelerated, Cross-Control, and Elevator Trim)

NOTE: The demonstrated stalls are not a proficiency requirement for private pilot certification. The purpose of the demonstrations is to help the student learn how to recognize, prevent, and if necessary, recover before the stall develops into a spin. These stalls should not be practiced without a qualified flight instructor. In addition, certain types of stalls might be prohibited in some airplanes.

REVIEW
❑ Airport, Runway, and Taxiway Signs, Markings, and Lighting
❑ Aviation Security
❑ Airspeed and Configuration Changes
❑ Flight at Approach Speed
❑ Flight at Various Airspeeds From Cruise to Slow Flight
❑ Climbing and Descending Turns (VR)
❑ Normal Takeoffs and Landings
❑ Collision Avoidance Procedures
❑ Traffic Patterns

COMPLETION STANDARDS
• Maintain coordinated airplane attitude control during basic maneuvers.
• Perform takeoffs without instructor assistance.
• Demonstrate correct communications and traffic pattern procedures.
• Complete landings with minimal instructor assistance.
• Demonstrate basic understanding of steep turns, slow flight, stalls, stall recovery, and emergency operations.
• Explain the causes and recovery procedures for secondary, accelerated, cross-control, and elevator-trim stalls, as well as spins.
• Indicate basic understanding of airplane control using the flight instruments.

POSTFLIGHT DEBRIEFING
- ❏ Critique maneuvers/procedures and SRM.
- ❏ Create a plan for skills that need improvement.
- ❏ Update the record folder and logbook.

STUDY ASSIGNMENT

Ground Lesson 6
Stage I Exam

Private Pilot Maneuvers Manual/EBook
Ground Reference Maneuvers

Maneuvers Lessons, Private Pilot Online — Jeppesen Learning Center
ML09 — Ground Reference Maneuvers

FLIGHT LESSON 5
DUAL — LOCAL (1.0)

NOTE: A view-limiting device is required for the 0.2 hours of dual instrument time allocated to Flight Lesson 5.

REFERENCES

Private Pilot Maneuvers Manual/EBook
Ground Reference Maneuvers

Private Pilot Online — Jeppesen Learning Center
Maneuvers Lesson 9 — Ground Reference Maneuvers

OBJECTIVES
- Practice the review maneuvers, including stalls and emergency landing procedures, to gain proficiency.
- Learn and practice ground reference maneuvers and maneuvering at slow airspeeds by instrument reference.

PREFLIGHT DISCUSSION
- ❏ Situational Awareness
- ❏ Realistic Distractions
- ❏ Determining Wind Direction
- ❏ Controlled Flight Into Terrain (CFIT) Awareness
- ❏ Wire Strike Avoidance

INTRODUCE
- ❏ Rectangular Courses
- ❏ S-Turns
- ❏ Turns Around a Point
- ❏ Maneuvering During Slow Flight (IR)

REVIEW

Slow flight should be practiced with realistic distractions and stall recovery practiced from straight flight and from turns.
- ❏ Maneuvering During Slow Flight (VR)
- ❏ Power-Off Stalls
- ❏ Power-On Stalls
- ❏ Spin Awareness
- ❏ Positive Exchange of Flight Controls
- ❏ Emergency Descent
- ❏ Emergency Approach and Landing (Simulated)
- ❏ Emergency Equipment and Survival Gear
- ❏ Normal Takeoffs and Landings
- ❏ Turns to Headings (IR)

COMPLETION STANDARDS

- Display increased proficiency in coordinated airplane attitude control during basic maneuvers.
- Perform takeoffs without instructor assistance.
- Demonstrate correct communications and traffic pattern procedures.
- Complete landings with minimal instructor assistance.
- Maintain altitude ± 225 feet and headings ± 15° during straight-and-level flight.
- Demonstrate understanding of the proper flight techniques and the appropriate wind correction techniques for flying rectangular courses, S-turns, and turns around a point.
- Demonstrate the ability to recognize and recover from stalls.
- Indicate basic understanding of attitude instrument flying and simulated emergency landing procedures.

POSTFLIGHT DEBRIEFING

- ❏ Critique maneuvers/procedures and SRM.
- ❏ Create a plan for skills that need improvement.
- ❏ Update the record folder and logbook.

STUDY ASSIGNMENT

Ground Lesson 7
Meteorology for Pilots

Private Pilot Maneuvers Manual/EBook
Airport Operations

Maneuvers Lessons, Private Pilot Online — Jeppesen Learning Center
ML10 — Traffic Patterns
ML14 — Normal Takeoff and Climb
ML15 — Normal Approach and Landing
ML16 — Crosswind Takeoff and Landing

FLIGHT LESSON 6
DUAL — LOCAL (1.0)

REFERENCES

 Private Pilot Maneuvers Manual/EBook
Airport Operations

 Private Pilot Online — Jeppesen Learning Center
Maneuvers Lessons 10, 14, 15, 16 — Airport Operations

OBJECTIVES
- Practice the review maneuvers, including ground reference maneuvers, to gain proficiency.
- Learn how to conduct go-arounds, slips, and crosswind takeoffs and landings in varying wind conditions. Review procedures for runway incursion avoidance, learn about land and hold short operations (LAHSO), and wake turbulence avoidance.

PREFLIGHT DISCUSSION
- ❏ Communication
- ❏ Workload Management
- ❏ Lost Communication Procedures
- ❏ Runway Incursion Avoidance
- ❏ Land and Hold Short Operations (LAHSO)
- ❏ Wake Turbulence Avoidance

INTRODUCE
- ❏ Go-Around/Rejected Landing Forward Slips to Landing
- ❏ Crosswind Takeoff and Climb
- ❏ Crosswind Approach and Landing
- ❏ ATC Light Signals
- ❏ Land and Hold Short Operations (LAHSO)
- ❏ Wake Turbulence Avoidance

REVIEW
- ❏ Runway Incursion Avoidance
- ❏ Rectangular Courses
- ❏ S-Turns
- ❏ Turns Around a Point
- ❏ Normal Takeoffs and Landings
- ❏ Traffic Patterns
- ❏ Emergency Approach and Landing (Simulated)
- ❏ Controlled Flight Into Terrain (Discussion Only)

STAGE I ■ **Flight Training Syllabus**

COMPLETION STANDARDS
- Maintain coordinated airplane attitude control.
- Fly a specific ground track while maintaining altitude ± 200 feet.
- Demonstrate basic understanding of how the forward slip is used for an approach to a landing.
- Explain crosswind takeoff/landing procedures and go-arounds.
- Explain procedures for runway incursion avoidance, land and hold short operations (LAHSO), and wake turbulence avoidance.

POSTFLIGHT DEBRIEFING
- ❏ Critique maneuvers/procedures and SRM.
- ❏ Create a plan for skills that need improvement.
- ❏ Update the record folder and logbook.

STUDY ASSIGNMENT

Ground Lesson 8
Federal Aviation Regulations

Private Pilot Maneuvers Manual/EBook
Review Maneuvers 1 - 14

Maneuvers Lessons, Private Pilot Online — Jeppesen Learning Center
Review Maneuvers 1 - 16

FLIGHT LESSON 7
DUAL — LOCAL (1.0)
NOTE: A view-limiting device is required for the 0.2 hours of dual instrument time allocated to Flight Lesson 7

REFERENCES

Private Pilot Maneuvers Manual/EBook
Review Maneuvers 1 - 14

Private Pilot Online — Jeppesen Learning Center
Maneuvers 1 - 16

OBJECTIVES
Prepare for the first solo flight by demonstrating proficiency in:
- Conducting flight maneuvers, takeoffs, landings, go-arounds, and emergency procedures.
- Flying by reference to instruments
- Flying ground reference maneuvers.

PREFLIGHT DISCUSSION
- ❏ Sections of FAR Parts 61 and 91 that apply to private pilots

❑ Airspace rules and procedures for the airport where solo flight will be performed

❑ Flight characteristics and operational limitations for the make and model of aircraft to be flown in solo flight

❑ SRM—Aeronautical Decision Making

REVIEW

❑ Straight-and-Level Flight (VR/IR)
❑ Constant Airspeed Climbs (VR/IR)
❑ Constant Airspeed Descents (VR/IR)
❑ Climbing and Descending Turns (VR/IR)
❑ Turns to Headings (VR/IR)
❑ Steep Turns
❑ Rectangular Courses
❑ Turns Around a Point
❑ Crosswind Takeoff and Climb
❑ Crosswind Approach and Landing
❑ Runway Incursion Avoidance
❑ Land and Hold Short Operations (LAHSO)
❑ Wake Turbulence Avoidance
❑ Go-Around/Rejected Landing
❑ Forward Slips to Landing
❑ Systems and Equipment Malfunctions
❑ ATC Light Signals
❑ Emergency Approach and Landing (Simulated)

COMPLETION STANDARDS

- Display increased proficiency and skill in instrument scan and interpretation during practice of instrument flight maneuvers.
- Perform takeoffs, landings, and go-arounds at a safe airspeed without instructor assistance
- Perform emergency procedures with minimal instructor assistance.
- Display increasing proficiency and precision when performing ground reference maneuvers.

POSTFLIGHT DEBRIEFING

❑ Critique maneuvers/procedures and SRM.
❑ Create a plan for skills that need improvement.
❑ Update the record folder and logbook.

STUDY ASSIGNMENT

Ground Lesson 9
Interpreting Weather Data

Prepare for the Presolo Exam and Briefing. The student will be provided with the exam questions in advance.

FLIGHT LESSON 8
DUAL — LOCAL (1.0)

NOTE: A view-limiting device is required for the 0.2 hours of dual instrument time allocated to Flight Lesson 8.

NOTE: Presolo briefing questions are included in the Appendix.

OBJECTIVES
- Grade the Presolo Exam and conduct the Presolo Briefing.
- Practice the listed review maneuvers, procedures, and emergency operations and basic instrument maneuvers, to gain proficiency and confidence.
- Correct of any faulty tendencies and prepare for the first solo.

PREFLIGHT DISCUSSION
❏ Presolo Exam Critique
❏ Presolo Flight Training Requirements

REVIEW
❏ Operation of Systems
❏ Preflight Inspection
❏ Engine Starting
❏ Radio Communication
❏ Normal and Crosswind Taxiing
❏ Before-Takeoff Check
❏ Normal and Crosswind Takeoff
❏ Positive Aircraft Control
❏ Climbing and Descending Turns
❏ Collision Avoidance Procedures
❏ Straight-and-Level Flight (IR)
❏ Turns to Headings (IR)
❏ Maneuvering During Slow Flight (IR)
❏ Power-Off Stalls
❏ Power-On Stalls
❏ Maneuvering During Slow Flight
❏ Flight at Slow Airspeeds with Realistic Distractions, and the Recognition and Recovery from Stalls Entered from Straight Flight and from Turns
❏ Spin Awareness
❏ Steep Turns
❏ Rectangular Courses
❏ S-Turns
❏ Turns Around a Point
❏ Systems and Equipment Malfunctions
❏ Emergency Procedures
❏ Emergency Approach and Landing (Simulated)
❏ Traffic Patterns
❏ Forward Slips to Landing
❏ Go-Around/Rejected Landing
❏ Runway Incursion Avoidance
❏ Land and Hold Short Operations (LAHSO)

❑ Wake Turbulence Avoidance
❑ Normal and Crosswind Approach and Landing

COMPLETION STANDARDS
- Successfully pass the Presolo Exam with a minimum score of 80%, and review with the instructor each incorrect response to ensure complete understanding.
- Demonstrate ability and readiness for solo flight in the traffic pattern.
- Consistently perform takeoffs and climbs, approaches and landings, and go-arounds safely and without instructor assistance
- Exhibit understanding of attitude instrument flying and be able to control the airplane by instrument reference.
- Explain local airport and airspace rules.
- Explain how to handle systems and equipment malfunctions and related emergency procedures.

POSTFLIGHT DEBRIEFING
❑ Critique maneuvers/procedures and SRM.
❑ Create a plan for skills that need improvement.
❑ Update the record folder and logbook.

STUDY ASSIGNMENT

Review any deficient subject areas based on the results of the Presolo Exam. Review *Private Pilot Maneuvers* and *Maneuvers* software course as required, or as assigned by the instructor.

FLIGHT LESSON 9
DUAL — LOCAL (0.5)
SOLO — LOCAL (0.5)

NOTE: This flight becomes the first flight lesson in Stage II if the Stage I Check precedes the first solo. If that is the case, proceed directly to Flight Lesson 10, the Stage I Check.

NOTE: Student pilots conducting solo flight operations are not authorized to participate in LAHSO.

OBJECTIVES
- During the dual portion of the lesson, the instructor reviews takeoff and landing procedures and ensure the student's readiness for solo flight.
- During the second portion of the lesson, the student conducts the first supervised solo flight in the local traffic pattern.
- Ensure consistent performance of the correct procedures and techniques for the student's first solo.

PREFLIGHT DISCUSSION
❑ Student questions
❑ Student pilot supervised solo flight operations in the local traffic pattern

STAGE I ■ **Flight Training Syllabus**

❑ Aeronautical Decision Making
❑ Task Management

REVIEW

DUAL
❑ Engine Starting
❑ Radio Communications
❑ Taxiing
❑ Before-Takeoff Check
❑ Normal Takeoff and Climb
❑ Traffic Patterns
❑ Go-Around/Rejected Landing
❑ Normal Approach and Landing

INTRODUCE

SUPERVISED SOLO
❑ Radio Communications
❑ Taxiing
❑ Before-Takeoff Check
❑ Normal Takeoffs and Climbs (3)
❑ Traffic Patterns (3)
❑ Normal Approaches and Landings (3)
❑ After Landing, Parking, and Securing

COMPLETION STANDARDS
• Display the ability to solo the training airplane safely in the traffic pattern. At no time will the safety of the flight be in question.
• Complete solo flight in the local traffic pattern as directed by the instructor.

POSTFLIGHT DEBRIEFING
❑ Critique maneuvers/procedures and SRM.
❑ Create a plan for skills that need improvement.
❑ Update the record folder and logbook.

STUDY ASSIGNMENT

Ground Lesson 10

Stage II Exam Review, as required, in preparation for the Stage I Check in Flight Lesson 10.

NOTE: If this is the first flight in Stage II, complete the study assignment for performance takeoffs and landings in Flight Lesson 11.

FLIGHT LESSON 10
DUAL — LOCAL (1.0)
STAGE I CHECK

OBJECTIVES
- Demonstrate to the chief instructor, the assistant chief instructor, or the designated check instructor that you are prepared to depart the traffic pattern area on future solo flights.
- In addition demonstrate proficiency in other maneuvers, procedures, and knowledge areas required to complete the first stage of flight training.

PREFLIGHT DISCUSSION
Conduct of the Stage I Check, including:
- ❏ Maneuvers
- ❏ Procedures
- ❏ Acceptable Performance Criteria
- ❏ Applicable Rules

EVALUATE
- ❏ Operation of Systems
- ❏ Airworthiness Requirements
- ❏ Engine Starting
- ❏ Radio Communications
- ❏ Taxiing
- ❏ Before-Takeoff Check
- ❏ Normal and Crosswind Takeoff and Climb
- ❏ Collision Avoidance Procedures
- ❏ Wake Turbulence Avoidance
- ❏ Maneuvering During Slow Flight
- ❏ Flight at Slow Airspeeds with Realistic Distractions, and the Recognition and Recovery from Stalls Entered from Straight Flight and from Turns
- ❏ Spin Awareness
- ❏ Power-Off Stalls
- ❏ Power-On Stalls
- ❏ Systems and Equipment Malfunctions
- ❏ Emergency Procedures
- ❏ Emergency Descent
- ❏ Emergency Approach and Landing (Simulated)
- ❏ Traffic Patterns
- ❏ Normal and Crosswind Approach and Landing

COMPLETION STANDARDS
This lesson and Stage I are complete when the student can competently perform preflight duties and all other procedures and maneuvers necessary for the safe conduct of a solo flight in the local training area. The student will maintain altitude ± 150 feet, headings ± 15°, and airspeed ± 10 knots.

POSTFLIGHT DEBRIEFING

❏ Evaluate maneuvers/procedures and SRM.

❏ Plan further instruction for skills not meeting Stage I completion standards.

❏ Update the record folder and logbook.

STUDY ASSIGNMENT

Ground Lesson 11
Airplane Performance

Private Pilot Maneuvers Manual/EBook
Performance Takeoffs and Landings

Maneuvers Lessons, Private Pilot Online — Jeppesen Learning Center
Private ML17 — Short- and Soft-Field Takeoffs and Landings

Stage II

STAGE OBJECTIVES

During Stage II, the student expands the skills learned in the previous stage. The student is introduced to short-field and soft-field takeoff and landing procedures, as well as night flying, which are important steps in preparation for cross-country training. Additionally, greater emphasis is placed on attitude control by instrument reference to increase the student's overall competence. In the cross-country phase, the student will learn to effectively plan and conduct cross-country flights in the National Airspace System using pilotage, dead reckoning, and VOR, GPS, and ADF navigation systems (based on aircraft equipment).

STAGE COMPLETION STANDARDS

At the completion of Stage II, the student will have successfully completed the first solo (if the first solo flight lesson occurs in this stage). In addition, the student will be able to accurately plan and conduct cross-country flights and be able to safely and consistently perform short-field and soft-field takeoffs and landings and carry out night operations. The proficiency level must be such that the successful and safe outcome of each task is never in doubt.

FLIGHT LESSON 11
DUAL — LOCAL (1.0)

REFERENCES

Private Pilot Maneuvers Manual/EBook
Performance Takeoffs and Landings

Private Pilot Online — Jeppesen Learning Center
Maneuvers Lesson 17

OBJECTIVES
- Learn the basic procedures for short- and soft-field takeoffs, climbs, approaches, and landings in the training airplane.
- Review ground reference maneuvers, slow flight, and stall recognition.
- Ensure that the student is confident and competent to fly the second supervised solo in the traffic pattern.

PREFLIGHT DISCUSSION
❑ Single-Pilot Resource Management (SRM)
❑ Risk Management
❑ Weight and Balance Computations
❑ Performance Estimates

STAGE II ■ Flight Training Syllabus

43

❑ Effects of High Density Altitude
❑ Aeronautical Decision Making
❑ Pilot-in-Command Responsibility

INTRODUCE

❑ Special Use Airspace
❑ Temporary Flight Restrictions (TFRs)
❑ Low-Level Wind Shear Precautions
❑ Short-Field Takeoff and Maximum-Performance Climb
❑ Soft-Field Takeoff and Climb
❑ Short-Field Approach and Landing
❑ Soft-Field Approach and Landing

REVIEW

❑ Aviation Security
❑ Rectangular Courses
❑ Turns Around a Point
❑ S-Turns
❑ Maneuvering During Slow Flight
❑ Stalls (Power-Off, and Power-On)

COMPLETION STANDARDS

- Explain the precautions to be taken when low-level wind shear is expected.
- Explain the runway conditions that necessitate the use of soft-field and short-field takeoff and landing techniques.
- Demonstrate understanding of the correct procedures for short- and soft-field takeoffs and landings, and perform them with instructor assistance.
- Perform ground reference maneuvers with an accurate ground track, maintaining altitude ± 150 feet.

POSTFLIGHT DEBRIEFING

❑ Critique maneuvers/procedures and SRM.
❑ Create a plan for skills that need improvement.
❑ Update the record folder and logbook.

STUDY ASSIGNMENT

Ground Lesson 12
Navigation

Review, as required, in preparation for Flight Lesson 12, which is the second supervised solo in the traffic pattern

FLIGHT LESSON 12
SOLO— LOCAL (1.0)

NOTE: At the instructor's discretion, a portion of this lesson may be dual.

NOTE: Student pilots conducting solo flight operations are not authorized to participate in LAHSO.

OBJECTIVES
- Fly the second supervised solo in the local traffic pattern.
- Gain confidence in conducting airport operations, including takeoff, traffic pattern, approach and landing procedures, as well as collision avoidance and radio communications.

PREFLIGHT DISCUSSION
❏ SRM—Situational Awareness
❏ Solo Operations in the Traffic Pattern

REVIEW

SUPERVISED SOLO
❏ Radio Communications
❏ Taxiing
❏ Before-Takeoff Check
❏ Normal Takeoff and Climb
❏ Traffic Patterns
❏ Normal Approach and Landing
❏ After Landing, Parking, and Securing

COMPLETION STANDARDS
- Perform takeoffs using the correct techniques with liftoff speed within ± 5 knots.
- Perform stabilized approaches to landing with approach speed within ± 5 knots.
- Perform each landing touchdown at the correct speed within 300 feet of the desired touchdown point.

POSTFLIGHT DEBRIEFING
❏ Critique maneuvers/procedures and SRM.
❏ Create a plan for skills that need improvement.
❏ Update the record folder and logbook.

STUDY ASSIGNMENT
Ground Lesson 13
Human Factor Principles

Review, as required, in preparation for the first solo flight in the local flying area.

STAGE II ■ Flight Training Syllabus

FLIGHT LESSON 13
SOLO — LOCAL (1.0)

OBJECTIVES
- Practice ground reference maneuvers to increase skill in maintaining specific ground tracks.
- Gain proficiency and confidence conducting other maneuvers listed for review.
- Practice other maneuvers as directed by the flight instructor.
- Improve skills in traffic pattern entry, exit, approach, and landing procedures, including use of a stabilized approach.

REVIEW
- ❏ Radio Communications
- ❏ Normal and Crosswind Takeoffs and Climbs
- ❏ Power-Off Stalls
- ❏ Power-On Stalls
- ❏ Maneuvering During Slow Flight
- ❏ S-Turns
- ❏ Turns Around a Point
- ❏ Traffic Patterns
- ❏ Normal and Crosswind Approaches and Landings

COMPLETION STANDARDS
- Safely conduct the assigned solo flight.
- Demonstrate proficiency in each of the assigned maneuvers and procedures.

POSTFLIGHT DEBRIEFING
- ❏ Critique maneuvers/procedures and SRM.
- ❏ Create a plan for skills that need improvement.
- ❏ Update the record folder and logbook.

STUDY ASSIGNMENT

Ground Lesson 14
Flying Cross Country

Private Pilot Maneuvers Manual/EBook
Attitude Instrument Flying

Maneuvers Lessons, Private Pilot Online — Jeppesen Learning Center
Review ML08 — Attitude Instrument Flying

FLIGHT LESSON 14
DUAL — LOCAL (1.0)

NOTE: A view-limiting device is required for the 0.5 hours of dual instrument time allocated to Flight Lesson 14.

REFERENCES

Private Pilot Maneuvers Manual/EBook
Attitude Instrument Flying

Private Pilot Online — Jeppesen Learning Center
Maneuvers Lesson 8

OBJECTIVES

- Practice the listed maneuvers to gain proficiency and confidence.
- Gain proficiency in attitude instrument flying and control the airplane by instrument reference during simulated emergency situations.
- Begin navigating using VOR, GPS, and ADF navigation (based on aircraft equipment).

PREFLIGHT DISCUSSION

- ❑ Basic Instrument Maneuvers
- ❑ Recovery from Unusual Flight Attitudes
- ❑ Radio Communication, Navigation Systems/Facilities, and Radar Services
- ❑ Resource Use
- ❑ Situational Awareness
- ❑ Disorientation

INTRODUCE

- ❑ VOR Orientation and Tracking (VR)
- ❑ GPS Orientation and Tracking (VR)
- ❑ ADF Orientation and Homing (VR)
- ❑ Power-Off Stalls (IR)
- ❑ Power-On Stalls (IR)
- ❑ Recovery from Unusual Flight Attitudes (IR)
- ❑ Using Radio Communications, Navigation Systems/Facilities, and Radar Services (IR)
- ❑ Basic Autopilot Use (if equipped) (VR/IR)

REVIEW

- ❑ Low-Level Wind Shear Precautions
- ❑ Short-Field Takeoffs and Maximum Performance Climbs
- ❑ Short-Field Approaches and Landings
- ❑ Power-Off Stalls
- ❑ Power-On Stalls
- ❑ Maneuvering During Slow Flight (IR)

COMPLETION STANDARDS

- Perform takeoffs and landings smoothly, maintaining directional control.
- Perform stabilized approaches to landing maintaining the proper airspeed within ± 5 knots.

STAGE II ■ **Flight Training Syllabus**

- Demonstrate basic understanding of VOR, GPS, and ADF navigation.
- Display the correct unusual attitude recovery techniques.

POSTFLIGHT DEBRIEFING
❑ Critique maneuvers/procedures and SRM.
❑ Create a plan for skills that need improvement.
❑ Update the record folder and logbook.

STUDY ASSIGNMENT
Ground Lesson 15
Stage III Exam

FLIGHT LESSON 15
DUAL — LOCAL (1.0)
NOTE: A view-limiting device is required for the 0.5 hours of dual instrument time allocated to Flight Lesson 15.

OBJECTIVES
- Gain proficiency in attitude instrument flying
- Learn how to use basic instrument skills to manage marginal VFR conditions or turn back to VFR conditions after inadvertent flight into IFR conditions.
- Review short- and soft-field procedures and emergency operations.

PREFLIGHT DISCUSSION
❑ Flight Instrument Functions, Common Errors, and Limitations
❑ Navigation Instruments
❑ Inadvertent Flight into IFR Conditions
❑ Operations in Turbulence
❑ Partial Panel
❑ Resource Use

REVIEW
❑ Autopilot Use (if equipped) (VR/IR)
❑ VOR Orientation and Tracking (VR/IR)
❑ GPS Orientation and Tracking (VR/IR)
❑ ADF Orientation and Homing (VR/IR)
❑ Maneuvering During Slow Flight (VR/IR)
❑ Power-Off Stalls (VR/IR)
❑ Power-On Stalls (VR/IR)
❑ Using Radio Communication, Navigation Systems/Facilities, and Radar Services (IR)
❑ Recovery From Unusual Flight Attitudes (IR)
❑ Short-Field Takeoffs/Maximum Performance Climbs and Landings
❑ Soft-Field Takeoffs and Landings
❑ Crosswind Takeoffs and Landings
❑ Forward Slips to a Landing
❑ Go-Around/Rejected Landing
❑ Emergency Operations

COMPLETION STANDARDS
- Demonstrate competency in basic instrument maneuvers and procedures, including control of the airplane during recovery from unusual flight attitudes.
- Control altitude ± 150 feet during level turns, straight-and-level flight, and slow flight.
- Recover promptly from fully-developed stalls, using the correct techniques and maintaining coordinated flight.
- Demonstrate increasing skill in short- and soft-field takeoffs and landings.

POSTFLIGHT DEBRIEFING
- ❑ Critique maneuvers/procedures and SRM.
- ❑ Create a plan for skills that need improvement.
- ❑ Update the record folder and logbook.

STUDY ASSIGNMENT
Private Pilot Maneuvers Manual/EBook
 Night Operations

Maneuvers Lessons, Private Pilot Online — Jeppesen Learning Center
 ML18 — Night Operations

FLIGHT LESSON 16
DUAL — NIGHT LOCAL (1.0)

NOTE: *The 10 night takeoffs and landings to a full stop with each involving flight in the traffic pattern are an FAR Part 141 requirement. Five are scheduled for Flight Lesson 16 and the other five for Flight Lesson 18. However, this requirement may be accomplished with fewer than five during a flight, as long as the total of 10 is completed.*

REFERENCES

Private Pilot Maneuvers Manual/EBook
 Night Operations

Private Pilot Online — Jeppesen Learning Center
 Maneuvers Lesson 18

OBJECTIVES
- Introduce the special operational considerations associated with night flying.
- Practice night takeoffs, climbs, traffic patterns, approaches and landings.
- Emphasize the physiological factors and additional planning associated with the night environment.

PREFLIGHT DISCUSSION
❏ Aeromedical Factors
❏ CFIT Awareness and Wire Strike Avoidance
❏ Visual Illusions and Disorientation
❏ Night Vision and Night Scanning/Collision Avoidance
❏ Aircraft, Airport, and Obstruction Lighting
❏ Personal Equipment

INTRODUCE
❏ Preparation for Night Flying
❏ Cockpit Management
❏ Flight Planning Considerations
❏ Use of Checklists
❏ Airworthiness Requirements
❏ Preflight Inspection
❏ Airport Lighting
❏ Taxiing
❏ Before-Takeoff Check
❏ Normal and Short-Field Takeoffs and Climbs
❏ VFR Navigation
❏ Steep Turns
❏ Maneuvering During Slow Flight
❏ Stalls–Power-Off and Power-On
❏ Normal and Short-Field Approaches and Landings
❏ Soft-Field Takeoffs and Landings
❏ Go-Around/Rejected Landing

COMPLETION STANDARDS
• Demonstrate understanding of the importance of attitude control.
• Control altitude ± 150 feet during level turns, straight-and-level flight, and slow flight. Stall recoveries should be coordinated with minimum altitude loss.
• Complete 5 takeoffs and landings to a full stop with each landing involving flight in the traffic pattern.
• Perform stabilized approaches to landing and touch down at a predetermined area on the runway.

POSTFLIGHT DEBRIEFING
❏ Critique maneuvers/procedures and SRM.
❏ Create a plan for skills that need improvement.
❏ Update the record folder and logbook.

STUDY ASSIGNMENT
Review, as required, in preparation for the dual cross-country in Flight Lesson 17.

FLIGHT LESSON 17
DUAL — CROSS-COUNTRY (2.0)

NOTE: A view-limiting device is required for the 0.5 hours of dual instrument time allocated to Flight Lesson 17.

NOTE: The flight must include a point of landing at a straight-line distance of more than 50 nautical miles from the original point of departure.

OBJECTIVES
- Introduce cross-country procedures and the proper techniques to be used during flights out of the local training area, including use of VOR, GPS, ADF, (based on aircraft equipment) and radar services under simulated instrument flight conditions.
- Prepare the student to make cross-country flights as the sole occupant of the airplane.
- Review instrument and emergency operations.
- Emphasize cross-country navigation procedures that include a point of landing at a straight-line distance of more than 50 nautical miles from the original point of departure.

PREFLIGHT DISCUSSION
❑ Aviation security
❑ National Airspace System

CROSS-COUNTRY FLIGHT PLANNING
❑ Special Use Airspace
❑ Temporary Flight Restrictions (TFRs)
❑ Sectional Charts
❑ Flight Publications
❑ Route Selection
❑ Pilotage and Dead Reckoning
❑ Weather Information
❑ Fuel Requirements
❑ Performance and Limitations
❑ Navigation Log
❑ FAA Flight Plan (How to Open, Close, or Amend)
❑ Weight and Balance
❑ Aeromedical Factors
❑ Single-Pilot Resource Management (SRM)
    ◊ Aeronautical Decision Making
    ◊ Risk Management
    ◊ Task Management

INTRODUCE

CROSS-COUNTRY FLIGHT
❑ Cockpit Management
❑ Flight Plan Considerations

STAGE II ▪ **Flight Training Syllabus**

❏ Departure
❏ Opening Flight Plan
❏ Course Interception
❏ Pilotage
❏ Dead Reckoning
❏ Radio Navigation (depending on aircraft equipment)
  ◊ VOR Navigation
  ◊ GPS Navigation
  ◊ ADF Navigation
❏ Autopilot Operation (if equipped)
❏ Use of Radar Services (VR)
❏ Power Settings and Mixture Control
❏ Diversion to an Alternate
❏ Lost Procedures
❏ Estimates of Groundspeed and ETA
❏ Position Fix by Navigation Facilities
❏ Flight on Federal Airways
❏ Collision Avoidance Procedures
❏ Closing the Flight Plan

INSTRUMENT FLIGHT
❏ Positive Aircraft Control
❏ Basic Instrument Maneuvers and Procedures
❏ Radio Navigation (based on aircraft equipment)
  ◊ VOR Navigation (IR)
  ◊ GPS Navigation (IR)
  ◊ ADF Navigation (IR)
❏ Use of Radar Services (IR)

AIRPORT OPERATIONS
❏ Controlled Airports
❏ Use of ATIS
❏ Use of Approach and Departure Control
❏ Go-Around/Rejected Landing
❏ CTAF/UNICOM Airports

REVIEW
❏ Runway Incursion Avoidance
❏ Emergency Operations
❏ Systems and Equipment Malfunctions
❏ Emergency Descent
❏ Emergency Approach and Landing (Simulated)
❏ Emergency Equipment and Survival Gear

COMPLETION STANDARDS:
• Demonstrate the skill to perform cross-country flight safely as the sole occupant of the airplane, including use of navigation systems and radar services under simulated instrument conditions.

- Complete at least one landing at a point that is a straight-line distance of more than 50 nautical miles from the original point of departure.
- Competently demonstrate complete preflight planning, weather analysis, use of FAA publications and charts, adherence to the preflight plan, and the use of pilotage, dead reckoning, radio communication, and navigation systems.

POSTFLIGHT DEBRIEFING
❏ Critique maneuvers/procedures and SRM.
❏ Create a plan for skills that need improvement.
❏ Update the record folder and logbook.

FLIGHT LESSON 18
DUAL — NIGHT CROSS-COUNTRY (2.0)

NOTE: A view-limiting device is required for the 0.5 hours of dual instrument time allocated to Flight Lesson 18.

NOTE: The flight must include a total distance of more than 100 nautical miles and a point of landing at a straight-line distance of more than 50 nautical miles from the original point of departure.

OBJECTIVES
- Perform night navigation, attitude instrument flying, and emergency operations.
- Learn the importance of thorough planning and accurate navigation.
- Fly the mission with precise aircraft control and navigate with the accuracy required to successfully complete a night VFR cross-country flight.

PREFLIGHT DISCUSSION
❏ Single-Pilot Resource Management
  ◊ Risk Management
  ◊ Task Management
  ◊ Situational Awareness
  ◊ CFIT Awareness
❏ Night Orientation, Navigation, and Chart Reading Techniques
❏ Weather Information
❏ Route Selection
❏ Altitude Selection
❏ Fuel Requirements
❏ Departure and Arrival Procedures

INTRODUCE
❏ Cockpit Management
❏ Pilotage
❏ Dead Reckoning
❏ VOR, GPS, and ADF Navigation (VR/IR) (based on aircraft equipment)
❏ Emergency Operations

- ❏ Use of Unfamiliar Airports
- ❏ Collision Avoidance Procedures
- ❏ Wire Strike Avoidance
- ❏ Diversion to Alternate
- ❏ Lost Procedures

REVIEW
- ❏ Preparation for Night Flight
- ❏ Aeromedical Factors
- ❏ Flight Plan Considerations
- ❏ Airport Lighting
- ❏ Normal and Short-Field Takeoffs and Climbs
- ❏ Autopilot Use
- ❏ Maneuvering During Slow Flight (VR/IR)
- ❏ Recovery from Unusual Flight Attitudes (IR)
- ❏ Normal and Short-Field Approaches and Landings
- ❏ Soft-Field Takeoffs and Landings
- ❏ Go-Around/Rejected Landing

COMPLETION STANDARDS
- Demonstrate understanding of night cross-country preparation and flight procedures, including the ability to maintain attitude by instrument reference.
- Navigate accurately and handle simulated emergency situations promptly, utilizing good judgment.
- Complete 5 takeoffs and landings to a full stop with each involving flight in the traffic pattern with one at least one landing at a point that is a straight-line distance of more than 50 NM from the original point of departure.
- Demonstrate stabilized approaches to landing with touchdown at or near the appropriate touchdown area on the runway.

POSTFLIGHT DEBRIEFING
- ❏ Critique maneuvers/procedures and SRM.
- ❏ Create a plan for skills that need improvement.
- ❏ Update the record folder and logbook.

STUDY ASSIGNMENT
Prepare for the Solo Cross-Country Briefing. (Refer to questions in the Appendix.)

FLIGHT LESSON 19
SOLO — CROSS-COUNTRY (2.5)

NOTE: This flight should include a point of landing that is at a straight-line distance of more than 50 nautical miles from the original point of departure.

NOTE: Solo Cross-Country Briefing questions are included in the Appendix.

OBJECTIVES
- Complete the Solo Cross-Country Briefing.
- Plan and fly a solo cross-country flight.
- Devise alternatives to use if the flight cannot be completed as planned.
- Increase proficiency and confidence in solo and cross-country operations.

PREFLIGHT DISCUSSION
- ❏ Solo Cross-Country Briefing Review
- ❏ Required Documents and Endorsements
- ❏ Basic VFR Weather Minimums and Airspace Rules
- ❏ Positive Aircraft Control
- ❏ Enroute Communication
- ❏ ATC Services
- ❏ Enroute Weather Information
- ❏ VFR Position Report
- ❏ Emergency Operations
- ❏ Lost Procedures
- ❏ Diversion
- ❏ Lost Communication Procedures
- ❏ ATC Light Signals
- ❏ Aeronautical Decision Making
- ❏ Resource Use
- ❏ Workload Management

REVIEW

PREFLIGHT PREPARATION
- ❏ Flight Plan Considerations
- ❏ National Airspace System
- ❏ Sectional Charts
- ❏ Flight Publications
- ❏ Route Selection
- ❏ Weather Information
- ❏ Fuel Requirements
- ❏ Performance and Limitations
- ❏ Weight and Balance
- ❏ Navigation Log
- ❏ FAA Flight Plan
- ❏ Aeromedical Factors

CROSS-COUNTRY FLIGHT
- ❏ Opening the Flight Plan
- ❏ VOR, GPS, and ADF Navigation (based on aircraft equipment)
- ❏ Position Fix by Navigation Facilities
- ❏ Pilotage
- ❏ Dead Reckoning
- ❏ Flight on Federal Airways

STAGE II ■ Flight Training Syllabus

❑ Use of Unfamiliar Airports
❑ Estimates of Groundspeed
❑ Estimates of ETA
❑ Closing the Flight Plan

COMPLETION STANDARDS

- Demonstrate accurate planning and conduct of a VFR cross-country flight, including accurate navigation.
- Exhibit an understanding of unfamiliar airport operations.
- Perform at least one landing more than 50 NM from the departure airport.

POSTFLIGHT DEBRIEFING

❑ Critique maneuvers/procedures and SRM.
❑ Create a plan for skills that need improvement.
❑ Update the record folder and logbook.

STUDY ASSIGNMENT

Ground Lessons 16 and 17
 Final Exams A and B

Review as required in preparation for the Stage II Check in Flight Lesson 20.,

FLIGHT LESSON 20
DUAL — LOCAL (1.0)
STAGE II CHECK

OBJECTIVES

- Demonstrate to the chief instructor, the assistant chief instructor, or the designated check instructor, proficiency in conducting takeoffs, landings, and stall recognition and recovery procedures.
- Demonstrate the ability to plan and conduct a cross-country flight, as well as safe and effective operation of the aircraft during all other phases of flight in Stages I and II of the Flight Training Syllabus.

PREFLIGHT DISCUSSION

Conduct of the Stage II Check, including:
❑ Maneuvers and Procedures
❑ Acceptable Performance Criteria
❑ Applicable Rules

EVALUATE

PREFLIGHT PREPARATION
❑ National Airspace System
❑ Cross-Country Planning
❑ Weather Information

❏ Cockpit Management
❏ Use of Checklists

CROSS-COUNTRY FLIGHT
❏ Positive Aircraft Control
❏ Stall/Spin Awareness
❏ Departure
❏ Course Interception
❏ VOR, GPS, and ADF Navigation (based on aircraft equipment)
❏ Pilotage and Dead Reckoning
❏ Collision Avoidance Procedures
❏ Diversion to Alternate
❏ Lost Procedures
❏ Emergency Operations
❏ Low Level Wind Shear Precautions
❏ Short-Field Takeoffs and Maximum Performance Climbs
❏ Short-Field Approaches and Landings
❏ Soft-Field Takeoffs and Climbs
❏ Soft-Field Approaches and Landings
❏ Stalls—Power-Off and Power-On

COMPLETION STANDARDS
• Demonstrate the ability to plan and conduct cross-country flights using sound knowledge of flight planning, preflight action, weather analysis, and the appropriate aeronautical publications.
• Exhibit the correct use of the methods of navigation, the ability to correctly determine location at any time, the ability to compute ETAs within 10 minutes, and the correct technique for establishing a course to an alternate airport.
• Demonstrate short- and soft-field takeoffs and landings safely and consistently.
• Demonstrate safe and efficient operation of the aircraft during the entire flight.
• Demonstrate proficiency in all other maneuvers and procedures, as well as the associated knowledge areas of Stages I and II prior to starting Stage III.

POSTFLIGHT DEBRIEFING
❏ Evaluate maneuvers/procedures and SRM.
❏ Plan further instruction for skills not meeting Stage II completion standards.
❏ Update the record folder and logbook.

STAGE II ■ **Flight Training Syllabus**

Stage III

STAGE OBJECTIVES
During this stage, the student will gain additional proficiency in solo cross-country operations and will receive instruction in preparation for the End-of-Course Flight Check.

STAGE COMPLETION STANDARDS
This stage will be complete when the student demonstrates performance of private pilot operations at a standard that meets or exceeds the minimum performance criteria established in the Airman Certification Standards for a private pilot certificate.

FLIGHT LESSON 21
SOLO — CROSS-COUNTRY (2.0)

NOTE: The flight must include a point of landing at a straight-line distance of more than 50 nautical miles from the original point of departure.

NOTE: The flight should include three takeoffs and landings to a full stop with each landing involving flight in the traffic pattern at an airport with an operating control tower. However, at the instructor's discretion, this solo training requirement may be completed in other flight lessons.

OBJECTIVES
- Complete the scheduled cross-country flight to improve judgment and confidence when operating in unfamiliar areas.
- Competently execute cross-country procedures and comply with rules for flight within Class D airspace.

PREFLIGHT DISCUSSION
- ❑ Required Documents and Endorsements
- ❑ Basic VFR Weather Minimums
- ❑ Route of Flight/Alternates, Emergency Operations
- ❑ Lost Procedures
- ❑ Diversion
- ❑ ETA Estimates
- ❑ Fuel Requirements
- ❑ Aeronautical Charts and Publications that Apply to the Flight
- ❑ Airspace Rules Pertinent to the Planned Route of Flight
- ❑ Enroute Communication, ATC Services, and Pertinent Sources of Weather Information
- ❑ Aeronautical Decision Making
- ❑ Situational Awareness

REVIEW

PREFLIGHT PREPARATION
- ❑ Aeronautical Decision-Making
- ❑ Task Management
- ❑ Situational Awareness
- ❑ Flight Plan Considerations
- ❑ National Airspace System
- ❑ Sectional Charts
- ❑ Flight Publications
- ❑ Route Selection
- ❑ Weather Information
- ❑ Fuel Requirements
- ❑ Performance and Limitations
- ❑ Weight and Balance
- ❑ Navigation Log
- ❑ FAA Flight Plan
- ❑ Aeromedical Factors

CROSS-COUNTRY FLIGHT
- ❑ Opening the Flight Plan
- ❑ Pilotage
- ❑ Dead Reckoning
- ❑ VOR, GPS, and ADF Navigation (based on aircraft equipment)
- ❑ Position Fix by Navigation Facilities
- ❑ Flight on Federal Airways Use of Unfamiliar Airports
- ❑ Estimates of Groundspeed and ETA
- ❑ Closing the Flight Plan

COMPLETION STANDARDS
- Safely complete the assigned cross-country flight.
- Revised in-flight ETAs at each checkpoint should not vary from the ATAs by more than ± 5 minutes.
- Perform at least one landing more than 50 NM from the departure airport.
- Complete three takeoffs and landings, with flight in the traffic pattern, at a controlled airport.

POSTFLIGHT DEBRIEFING
- ❑ Critique maneuvers/procedures and SRM.
- ❑ Create a plan for skills that need improvement.
- ❑ Update the record folder and logbook.

FLIGHT LESSON 22
SOLO — CROSS-COUNTRY (4.0)

NOTE: Due to the amount of time needed to complete this cross-country flight, the lesson may be conducted as two flights. If this is done, and in order for the flight to be classified as cross country, each flight must include a landing more than 50 NM from the departure airport.

NOTE: The flight should include three takeoffs and landings to a full stop with each landing involving flight in the traffic pattern at an airport with an operating control tower. However, at the instructor's discretion, this solo training requirement may be completed in other flight lessons.

OBJECTIVES
- Complete the long cross-country flight requirement, which includes a flight of at least 100 NM total distance, with landings at a minimum of three points, including a straight-line segment more than 50 nautical miles between takeoff and landing locations.
- Competently execute cross-country procedures and comply with rules for flight within Class D airspace.

PREFLIGHT DISCUSSION
❑ Conduct of the Planned Flight
❑ Cockpit Management, Decision Making, and Judgment
❑ FAA Flight Plan (How to Open, Close, or Amend)
❑ Emergency Operations
❑ Enroute Communications and Facilities
❑ In-Flight Weather Analysis
❑ Unfamiliar Airport Operations

REVIEW

PREFLIGHT PREPARATION
❑ Flight Planning Considerations
❑ National Airspace System
❑ Sectional Charts
❑ Flight Publications
❑ Route Selection
❑ Weather Information
❑ Fuel Requirements
❑ Performance and Limitations
❑ Weight and Balance
❑ Navigation Log
❑ FAA Flight Plan
❑ Aeromedical Factors

CROSS-COUNTRY FLIGHT
❑ Opening and Closing the Flight Plan
❑ VOR, GPS, and ADF Navigation (based on aircraft equipment)
❑ Pilotage
❑ Dead Reckoning
❑ Estimates of Groundspeed
❑ Estimates of ETA
❑ Use of Controlled Airports
❑ Use of CTAF/UNICOM Airports

COMPLETION STANDARDS
• Demonstrate cross-country proficiency by completing the flight as planned and without incident.
• Review the navigation log during the postflight evaluation to determine whether it was completed and used correctly.
• The cross-country flight must include a distance of over 100 NM with landings at a minimum of three points, including at least one segment of the flight consisting of straight-line distance of more than 50 NM between takeoff and landing locations.
• Successfully accomplish the three traffic pattern, takeoff, and landing requirements at a controlled airport (if not completed on previous solo flights).

POSTFLIGHT DEBRIEFING
❑ Critique maneuvers/procedures and SRM.
❑ Create a plan for skills that need improvement.
❑ Update the record folder and logbook.

FLIGHT LESSON 23
DUAL — LOCAL (2.0)

OBJECTIVES
• Review the areas of operation, including specified maneuvers and procedures assigned by the instructor to increase proficiency to the level required of a private pilot.
• Gain additional knowledge and skill in preparation for the private pilot practical test.
• Correct any deficient skill and knowledge areas.

PREFLIGHT DISCUSSION
Maneuvers and procedures in preparation for the Stage III Check, End-of-Course Flight Check, and FAA Practical Test, including spin awareness and night operations.

REVIEW

- ❑ Preflight Preparation
- ❑ Preflight Procedures
- ❑ Airport Operations
- ❑ Takeoffs—Normal, Crosswind, Short-Field, Soft-Field
- ❑ Cross-Country Flight Procedures
- ❑ Emergency Operations
- ❑ Basic Instrument Maneuvers (IR)
- ❑ Maneuvering During Slow Flight (VR/IR)
- ❑ Power-Off and Power-On Stalls (VR/IR)
- ❑ Steep Turns
- ❑ Ground Reference Maneuvers
- ❑ Using Radio Communications, Navigation Systems/Facilities, and Radar Services (IR)
- ❑ Recovery from Unusual Flight Attitudes (IR)
- ❑ Landings—Normal, Crosswind, Short-Field, Soft-Field
- ❑ Forward Slips to Landing
- ❑ Go-Around/Rejected Landing
- ❑ After Landing, Parking, and Securing
- ❑ Specific maneuvers or procedures assigned by the flight instructor

COMPLETION STANDARDS

Exhibit progress and acceptable proficiency by performing each assigned maneuver smoothly and with proper coordination and precision according to the criteria established by the Private Pilot Airman Certification Standards.

POSTFLIGHT DEBRIEFING

- ❑ Critique maneuvers/procedures and SRM.
- ❑ Create a plan for skills that need improvement.
- ❑ Update the record folder and logbook.

FLIGHT LESSON 24
DUAL — LOCAL (2.0)

OBJECTIVES

- Review the areas of operation specifically assigned by the instructor with special emphasis on correcting any deficiency in the performance of maneuvers or procedures before the Stage III Check.
- Further develop the student's knowledge and skill in preparation for the private pilot practical test.
- Refine SRM skills.

PREFLIGHT DISCUSSION

Maneuvers and procedures in preparation for the Stage III Check, End-of-Course Flight Check, and FAA Practical Test, including spin awareness and night operations

REVIEW

- ❏ Preflight Preparation
- ❏ Preflight Procedures
- ❏ Airport Operations
- ❏ Takeoffs—Normal, Crosswind, Short-Field, Soft-Field
- ❏ Cross-Country Flight Procedures
- ❏ Emergency Operations
- ❏ Basic Instrument Maneuvers (IR)
- ❏ Maneuvering During Slow Flight (VR/IR)
- ❏ Power-Off and Power-On Stalls (VR/IR)
- ❏ Steep Turns
- ❏ Ground Reference Maneuvers
- ❏ Using Radio Communications, Navigation Systems/Facilities, and Radar Services (IR)
- ❏ Recovery from Unusual Flight Attitudes (IR)
- ❏ Landings—Normal, Crosswind, Short-Field, Soft-Field
- ❏ Forward Slips to Landing
- ❏ Go-Around/Rejected Landing
- ❏ After Landing, Parking, and Securing
- ❏ Specific maneuvers or procedures assigned by the flight instructor

COMPLETION STANDARDS

- Exhibit competence and the ability to correct any weak performance areas determined previously.
- Perform each assigned maneuver and procedure with proper coordination and precision according to the criteria in the Private Pilot Airman Certification Standards.

POSTFLIGHT DEBRIEFING

- ❏ Critique maneuvers/procedures and SRM.
- ❏ Create a plan for skills that need improvement.
- ❏ Update the record folder and logbook.

FLIGHT LESSON 25
DUAL — LOCAL (1.0)
STAGE III CHECK

OBJECTIVES

- Demonstrate to the chief instructor, the assistant chief instructor, or the designated check instructor the ability to perform the listed maneuvers at the proficiency level of a private pilot.
- Demonstrate the ability to plan and safely conduct a cross-country flight.
- Demonstrate safe and efficient operation of the airplane during all phases of flight.
- Demonstrate effective single-pilot resource management skills.

PREFLIGHT DISCUSSION
Conduct of the Stage III Check, Including:
❏ Maneuvers and Procedures
❏ Acceptable Performance Criteria
❏ Applicable Rules
❏ Human Factors Concepts

EVALUATE
❏ Single-Pilot Resource Management

MANEUVERS AND PROCEDURES
❏ Preflight Preparation
❏ Preflight Procedures
❏ Airport Operations
❏ Takeoffs—Normal, Crosswind, Short-Field, Soft-Field
❏ Cross-Country Flight Procedures
❏ Emergency Operations
❏ Basic Instrument Maneuvers (IR)
❏ Maneuvering During Slow Flight (VR/IR)
❏ Power-Off and Power-On Stalls (VR/IR)
❏ Steep Turns
❏ Ground Reference Maneuvers
❏ Using Radio Communications, Navigation Systems/Facilities, and Radar Services (IR)
❏ Recovery from Unusual Flight Attitudes (IR)
❏ Landings—Normal, Crosswind, Short-Field, Soft-Field
❏ Forward Slips to Landing
❏ Go-Around/Rejected Landing After Landing, Parking, and Securing

CROSS-COUNTRY FLIGHT
❏ VOR, GPS, and ADF Navigation (VR/IR) (based on aircraft equipment)
❏ Pilotage and Dead Reckoning
❏ Diversion to Alternate
❏ Lost Procedures

COMPLETION STANDARDS
• Perform each maneuver and procedure at the proficiency level of a private pilot.
• Demonstrate mastery of the airplane so that the successful outcome of each task performed is never in doubt.
• Exhibit sound understanding of the knowledge, skill, and proficiency requirements for private pilot certification.
• Demonstrate the ability to plan and conduct cross-country flights using sound knowledge of flight planning, preflight action, weather analysis, and the appropriate aeronautical publications.
• Demonstrate effective single-pilot resource management skills.

POSTFLIGHT DEBRIEFING
❏ Critique maneuvers/procedures and SRM.
❏ Plan further instruction for skills not meeting Stage III completion standards.
❏ Update the record folder and logbook.

Any maneuvers or procedures which do not meet private pilot standards should be reviewed with the student and assigned additional practice.

STUDY ASSIGNMENT
Complete the Private Pilot Practical Test Briefing with the instructor in preparation for the End-of-Course Flight Check and the FAA Private Pilot Practical Test. Suggested questions for this briefing are included in the Appendix.

FLIGHT LESSON 26
DUAL — LOCAL (1.0)
END-OF-COURSE FLIGHT CHECK

OBJECTIVES
• Demonstrate to the chief instructor, the assistant chief instructor, or the designated check instructor, the overall proficiency, skill, and knowledge to obtain a private pilot certificate.
• Exhibit the sound judgment and decision making necessary for a private pilot to operate effectively and safely within the U.S. National Airspace System.

PREFLIGHT DISCUSSION
Conduct of the End-of-Course Flight Check, Including:
❏ Maneuvers
❏ Procedures
❏ Acceptable Performance Criteria
❏ Applicable Rules

EVALUATE

PREFLIGHT PREPARATION
❏ Certificates and Documents
❏ Airworthiness Requirements
❏ Weather Information
❏ Performance and Limitations
❏ Cross-Country Flight Planning
❏ Operation of Systems
❏ Aeromedical Factors

❏ National Airspace System

CROSS-COUNTRY FLYING
❑ Pilotage and Dead Reckoning
❑ VOR, GPS, and ADF Navigation (VR/IR) (based on aircraft equipment)
❑ Diversion to an Alternate
❑ Lost Procedures

PILOTING SKILLS
❑ Preflight Inspection
❑ Cockpit Management
❑ Checklists
❑ Engine Starting
❑ Taxiing
❑ Before-Takeoff Check
❑ Radio Communications
❑ ATC Light Signals
❑ Collision Avoidance Procedures
❑ Low-Level Wind Shear Precautions
❑ Wake Turbulence Avoidance
❑ Airport, Runway, and Taxiway Signs, Markings, and Lighting
❑ Normal and Crosswind Takeoffs and Climbs
❑ Short-Field Takeoff and Maximum-Performance Climb
❑ Soft-Field Takeoff and Climb
❑ Straight-and-Level Flight (VR/IR)
❑ Constant Airspeed Climbs (VR/IR)
❑ Constant Airspeed Descents (VR/IR)
❑ Turns to Headings (VR/IR)
❑ Recovery from Unusual Flight Attitudes (IR)
❑ Using Radio Communications, Navigation Facilities, and Radar Services (IR)
❑ Maneuvering During Slow Flight
❑ Power-Off Stalls
❑ Power-On Stalls
❑ Spin Awareness
❑ Steep Turns
❑ Ground Reference Maneuvers
❑ Emergency Descent
❑ Emergency Approach and Landing (Simulated)
❑ Emergency Equipment and Survival Gear
❑ Systems and Equipment Malfunctions
❑ Traffic Patterns
❑ Normal and Crosswind Approaches and Landings
❑ Forward Slips to Landing
❑ Go-Around/Rejected Landing
❑ Short-Field Approach and Landing
❑ Soft-Field Approach and Landing
❑ After Landing, Parking, and Securing

STAGE III ■ Flight Training Syllabus

COMPLETION STANDARDS

- Demonstrate proficiency that meets or exceeds the FAA Private Pilot Airman Certification Standards.
- Demonstrate mastery of the airplane so that the successful outcome of each task performed is never in doubt.
- Demonstrate effective single-pilot resource management skills.

POSTFLIGHT DEBRIEFING

- ❑ Evaluate maneuvers/procedures and SRM.
- ❑ Plan additional instruction for skills that do not meet course completion standards.
- ❑ Update the record folder and logbook.

STAGE III ■ **Flight Training Syllabus**

STAGE III ■ **Flight Training Syllabus**

Appendix — Pilot Briefing Questions

This appendix provides you with the necessary material to complete the presolo written exam and the pilot briefing sessions, or the tutoring sessions, which are assigned in the training syllabus. Each briefing is a series of questions designed to provide you with a systematic method of checking your student's knowledge level.

Each briefing should be completed before the appropriate flight lesson to gain optimum benefit. The session is not necessarily limited to the questions found in the briefing, since they may stimulate further questions in the same subject area. In addition, a checklist is provided to help you prepare your students for the FAA practical test.

PRESOLO EXAM BRIEFING

14 CFR Part 61.87 outlines the requirements for student pilot solo flights. As specified in this regulation, the student must demonstrate satisfactory knowledge of the required subject areas by completing a knowledge test.

This exam is to be administered and graded by the instructor who endorses the student pilot certificate for solo flight. Flight instructors must include questions on applicable portions of 14 CFR Parts 61 and 91. In addition, instructors should modify the written exam as necessary to make it appropriate for the aircraft to be flown and the local flying environment.

Students should complete the presolo knowledge exam using the booklet in their private pilot training kit. The questions are included here for instructor use.

GENERAL QUESTIONS

1. What personal documents and endorsements are you required to have before you fly solo? [FAR 61.87]
2. What are your student pilot limitations regarding carriage of passengers or cargo and flying for compensation or hire? [FAR 61.89]
3. Explain student pilot limitations concerning visibility and flight above clouds. [FAR 61.89]
4. Who has the final authority and responsibility for the operation of the airplane when you are flying solo? [FAR 1.1, 91.3, 91.7]
5. Discuss what preflight action concerning the airport and aircraft performance is specified in the regulations for a local flight. [FAR 91.103]
6. During engine runup, you cause rocks, debris, and propeller blast to be directed toward another aircraft or person. Could this be considered careless or reckless operations of an aircraft? [FAR 91.13]

7. You may not fly as pilot of a civil aircraft within _____ hours after consumption of any alcoholic beverage, or while having _____ % or greater of alcohol in your blood.. [91.17]

8. What are the general requirements pertaining to the use of safety belts and shoulder harnesses? [FAR 91.105, 91.107]

9. What is the minimum fuel reserve for day VFR flight, and on what cruise speed is the fuel reserve based? [FAR 91.151]

10. A transponder with Mode C is required at all times in all airspace at and above _____ feet MSL, except below _____ feet AGL. [FAR 91.215]

11. What aircraft certificates and documents must be on board when you are flying solo? [FAR 91.203, 91.9, 23.1519]

12. No person may operate an aircraft so close to another aircraft as to create an _____. [FAR 91.111]

13. Who has the right-of-way when two aircraft are on final approach to land at the same time? [FAR 91.113]

14. What action do you need to take if you are overtaking another aircraft and which aircraft has the right-of-way? What should you do if you are flying a head-on collision course with another aircraft? If another airplane is converging from the right, who has the right-of-way? [FAR 91.113]

15. Except when necessary for takeoffs and landings, what are the minimum safe altitudes when flying over congested and uncongested areas? [FAR 91.119]

16. If an altimeter setting is not available at an airport, what setting should you use before departing on a local flight? [FAR 91.121]

17. What altitudes should you use when operating under VFR in level cruising flight at more than 3,000 feet AGL? [FAR 91.159]

18. When practicing steep turns, stalls, and maneuvering during slow flight, the entry altitude must allow a recovery to be completed no lower than _____ feet AGL.

19. When is a go-around appropriate?

20. What general steps should you follow after an engine failure in flight?

AIRPLANE QUESTIONS

If necessary, the instructor may include additional questions pertaining to the make and model of airplane to be flown.

1. List the minimum equipment and instruments that must be working properly in your airplane for day VFR flight. [FAR 91.205]

2. Fill in the V-speed definitions and the corresponding speed for your airplane.

	Definition	**Speed**
V_{SO}	_____	_____
V_{S1}	_____	_____
V_X	_____	_____
V_Y	_____	_____

V_{FE} _____ _____

V_A _____ _____

V_{NO} _____ _____

V_{NE} _____ _____

3. What is the best glide speed for your training airplane?

4. What is the maximum allowable flap setting for takeoff in your airplane?

5. The total usable fuel capacity for your airplane is _____ gallons. On a standard day (sea level, temperature: 15°C, altimeter: 29.92 inches Hg), the fuel consumption rate during normal (approximately 75% power) cruise is _____ gallons per hour.

6. What grades of fuel can be safely used in your airplane? What are the colors of the recommended fuels? What happens to the color of the fuel if two grades are mixed?

7. The maximum oil capacity of your airplane is _____ quarts, and the minimum oil capacity to begin a flight is _____ quarts.

8. The maximum crosswind component specified by your instructor for solo takeoffs and landings in the training airplane is _____ knots. [FAR 61.89]

9. When do you use carburetor heat? What are the indications of carburetor icing?

10. What is the takeoff and landing distance over a 50-foot obstacle for your airplane at your airport? Assume maximum certificated takeoff weight, 80°F, winds calm, and an altimeter setting of 29.52.

AIRPORT AND LOCAL AIRSPACE QUESTIONS

Flight instructors may assign only those questions that pertain to the student's airport environment and surrounding local area. However, if necessary, instructors may assign additional questions for a particular flying area.

1. What are the traffic patterns for each runway at your airport? What is the MSL altitude for the traffic pattern?

2. How do you enter and exit the traffic pattern at your airport? What, if any, radio communications are required? [AIM] [AC 90-66]

3. What radio calls are recommended in the traffic pattern at an uncontrolled airport? What radio calls are required at your airport? [AIM]

4. What is the standard direction of turns in the traffic pattern? Give an example of a visual display indicating a nonstandard traffic pattern. [AIM]

5. What is CTAF? Explain CTAF procedures at your training airport(s). [AIM]

6. How can you determine if a runway is closed? [AIM]

7. What are the typical dimensions of Class D airspace and what requirement(s) must be met prior to entry? [FAR 91.129]

8. What is the maximum speed permitted for aircraft below 10,000 feet MSL? What is the maximum speed allowed in Class B airspace? What is the maximum speed allowed in a VFR corridor through Class B airspace? [FAR 91.117]

APPENDIX ■ Presolo Exam Briefing

9. If you receive ATC instructions that you feel may compromise safety or will cause you to violate an FAR, what should you do? [FAR 91.123]

10. What is the meaning of each of the following ATC light signals? [FAR 91.125]

SIGNAL	IN FLIGHT	ON THE GROUND
Steady green		N/A
Flashing green		
Flashing red		
Steady red		N/A

11. In addition to equipment requirements and a student pilot certificate, what other requirement(s), if any, must be met before a student pilot is authorized to fly solo within Class B airspace? [FAR 61.95]

12. Explain the general transponder equipment and use requirement(s) when operating within or near Class B airspace. [FAR 91.215]

13. Describe the Class B airspace boundaries that affect your airport, or an airport nearby. Explain how you can use navigation equipment and ground reference points to identify the Class B boundaries. (Draw a diagram, if necessary.)

14. You have called ATC just prior to entering the Class B airspace, and the controller tells you to, "Squawk 2466 and ident." Are you now allowed to enter the Class B airspace without any further instructions? Explain. [FAR 91.131]

15. On a sectional chart, what does a dashed magenta line around the airport indicate?

16. Explain the minimum visibility and ceiling requirements for VFR flight in Class D airspace.

17. May a student pilot request a special VFR clearance in Class D airspace when visibility is less than three miles? Explain your answer. [FAR 61.89, 91.157]

18. You have called ATC prior to entering Class C airspace, and the controller responds with your call sign and tells you to "Standby." Are you now allowed to enter this airspace without any further instructions? [AIM]

19. Describe the typical dimensions of Class C airspace. Is participation in the radar service mandatory within the outer area of Class C airspace?

20. Describe the Class C boundaries that affect your airport, or an airport nearby. Explain how you can use navigation equipment and ground reference points to identify the Class C inner and outer circles, as well as the outer area. (Draw a diagram, if necessary.)

SOLO CROSS-COUNTRY BRIEFING

Although the student has flown solo before the solo cross-country, regulations require that the student receive additional ground and flight instruction prior to conducting solo cross-country flight. The following briefing is designed to assist the instructor in determining if the student has an acceptable level of knowledge to conduct these operations safely.

1. Plan a cross-country flight by obtaining a weather briefing and completing a navigation log.
2. Select at least 10 examples of good checkpoints along your route of flight. Also, select at least 10 checkpoints that would be difficult to see from the air.
3. By referring to the chart used to plan the cross-country, determine all you can about the destination airport.
4. Where can you find additional information about the destination airport?
5. Can you buy fuel at your destination?
6. Explain how to determine your position by using VOR, ADF, or GPS, and how you can use these navigation systems to fly to your destination.
7. Once airborne, how will you open your flight plan?
8. If you find you are falling behind your ETA, what action should you take?
9. Upon arrival at your destination, how will you close your flight plan? [AIM]
10. If your flight plan is not closed, how long after your ETA will a search begin?
11. If you have a problem with the airplane enroute, where can you land?
12. Explain how to obtain current weather reports and forecasts while enroute. What will you do if the weather along your route of flight deteriorates? [AIM]
13. If you become lost, what will you do?
14. What are the minimum VFR fuel reserves required by FARs for day and night flight. [FAR 91.151]

PRIVATE PILOT PRACTICAL TEST BRIEFING

This is the last pilot briefing and one of the most important, because it prepares the student for the practical test. Remember that there isn't any formal division between the oral and flight portions of the practical test. Oral questioning can be used at any time to determine whether the student's knowledge of a subject area is adequate.

Your briefing of each student should be conducted on a private, individual basis in a manner similar to an actual practical test. The following sample questions indicate the types of questions an examiner might ask a candidate. Practical test preparation should include a discussion of 14 CFR Parts 61, 91, and NTSB 830, emphasizing the rules that apply to private pilots. You can also anticipate that the examiner will ask specific questions about the required flight maneuvers, as well as the airplane and its systems. A useful aid when preparing for oral questioning is your student's written test results. Discuss each incorrectly-answered FAA question subject, because the examiner is likely to emphasize these areas.

A useful aid when preparing for oral questioning is your student's written test results. Each FAA question incorrectly answered by the student should be thoroughly discussed, since the examiner may emphasize these areas.

APPENDIX ■ Presolo Exam Briefing

AIRCRAFT CERTIFICATES AND DOCUMENTS

1. What documents must be on board the aircraft before operation? Where are they normally located?
2. Who is responsible for determining whether an aircraft is safe for flight?
3. Must the engine and aircraft logbooks be carried on board the aircraft? [91.417]
4. Locate the last annual inspection in the aircraft logbooks and determine when the next inspection is due. [FAR 91.409]
5. If the engine logbook does not reflect a current annual inspection but the aircraft logbook does, is the aircraft legal for operation?
6. When is a 100-hour inspection required?
7. If the aircraft has a transponder, locate its last inspection in the logbook. When is its next inspection due? [FAR 91.413]
8. If an airplane is equipped with a transponder and the aircraft logbook indicates the inspection has expired, can the transponder still be used? [FAR 91.413]
9. Describe the items that you can use to determine the operating limitations of the aircraft. [FAR 91.9]
10. Where can you find the aircraft's empty weight and moment? What is the empty weight and moment for your airplane?

AIRPLANE SYSTEMS

1. What is the minimum grade of fuel required for operation of your airplane? What color is the fuel?
2. If the specified grade of fuel is not available, should you use a lower or higher than normal grade? Why?
3. What is the total fuel capacity of the aircraft? How much fuel is unusable?
4. Where is the fuel selector located? What is the correct procedure for switching fuel tanks, if appropriate?
5. What is the purpose of an auxiliary electric fuel pump? When should you use it?
6. What is the purpose of the fuel tank quick drains?
7. What is the purpose of the fuel tank vent?
8. When should you check the fuel tanks for fuel contamination?
9. What are some ways to reduce the possibility of fuel contamination?
10. What is the electrical system voltage when the alternator is running? What is the battery voltage?
11. Does your airplane have a generator or an alternator? Does it produce alternating current (AC) or direct current (DC)?
12. What are the basic advantages of an alternator over a generator?
13. What is the purpose of the voltage regulator?
14. How do you detect alternator or generator failure?

15. Why is an ammeter or load meter installed in the airplane, and what does each indicate?

16. Is the electrical system protected by circuit breakers or fuses?

17. What is the procedure for resetting a tripped circuit breaker?

18. Describe how you should use the primer during cold and warm weather operations.

19. After priming the engine during a cold weather start, is it advisable to "pump" the throttle after engaging the starter? Explain.

20. During a cold weather start, the oil pressure gauge does not indicate any oil pressure for nearly 30 seconds. What should you do?

21. During the magneto check before takeoff, when you switch from BOTH to the RIGHT position, the rpm remains the same as it was in the BOTH position. Does this mean that the aircraft has an exceptionally good magneto? Explain.

22. Is it possible for carburetor icing to develop during a taxi operation? Explain.

23. Should you normally use carburetor heat during the takeoff? Explain.

24. What might cause engine roughness during runup at a high elevation field (5,000 feet MSL) during hot weather? What action is appropriate in this situation?

25. What is the first indication of carburetor icing on an airplane with a fixed-pitch or a constant-speed propeller?

26. What methods should you use to decrease or prevent engine overheating during climbs?

27. Describe the technique to achieve a lean fuel mixture during cruise flight.

28. Define the term "basic empty weight."

29. Is it acceptable to use the empty weight posted in the pilot's operating handbook sample problem for weight and balance computations? Explain.

30. What is the "reference datum?" Where is it located on this aircraft?

31. Define the term "allowable center of gravity (or moment) range." [FAA-H-8083-1 Aircraft Weight and Balance Handbook]

32. What is the center of gravity (or moment) range for your training airplane at its maximum takeoff weight?

33. Compute a weight and balance problem for the actual flight test conditions. Does the center of gravity (or moment) fall within limits?

34. What flight characteristics may you expect if the aircraft is loaded with the CG too far forward or too far aft?

35. What is the maximum allowable baggage weight if the CG is within the center of gravity envelope?

36. How do you know if the weight and balance data of the airplane have been changed? How is the change and the nature of the modification recorded?

APPENDIX ■ Presolo Exam Briefing

PERFORMANCE

1. Indicate 5 to 10 factors that can affect takeoff distance.

2. Compute the density altitude given the following conditions:
   ◊ Field elevation: 5,000 ft
   ◊ Altimeter: 30.12 inches Hg
   ◊ Outside air temperature: 35°C

Use the pilot's operating handbook of the airplane you will use for the practical test to answer questions 3 through 9.

3. Given the following conditions, compute the takeoff distance.
   ◊ Runway: Hard surfaced
   ◊ Flaps: Up
   ◊ Aircraft weight: Maximum takeoff
   ◊ Headwind: 10 knots
   ◊ Field elevation: 4,000 ft
   ◊ Outside air temperature: 29°C

4. Given the following conditions, determine the landing distance.
   ◊ Field elevation: 3,000 ft
   ◊ Outside air temperature: 10°C
   ◊ Headwind: 10 knots
   ◊ Aircraft weight: Maximum landing

5. Assume you depart an airport that is at sea level and climb to a cruising altitude of 8,500 feet. Calculate the time, fuel, and distance you will need to complete the climb.

6. During a short-field landing, what technique provides maximum braking effectiveness?

7. When landing on a sod runway, should you expect a longer or a shorter than normal landing roll? What should you expect on a runway covered with water, snow, or slush?

8. Define best angle-of-climb and best rate-of-climb airspeed. What are these airspeeds for your airplane?

9. How do you convert indicated to calibrated airspeed? Is this conversion necessary during normal operations?

LIMITATIONS

1. Under which category is your airplane certificated? Are spins approved?

2. What is the maximum positive G-loading approved in this airplane with the flaps up? What is the maximum G-loading with flaps down?

3. State the V-speed value of each color code on the airspeed indicator and define its meaning and significance.

	Speed	Definition
◊ White	_____	_____
◊ Green	_____	_____
◊ Yellow	_____	_____
◊ Red	_____	_____

4. Define maneuvering speed and its significance to the airplane. Is this speed designated by a colored marking on the airspeed indicator?

5. What other airspeed limitations exist for this airplane?

6. What are the maximum takeoff and landing weights for this airplane?

WEATHER AND CROSS-COUNTRY FLIGHT PLANNING

1. How can you obtain weather reports and forecasts? Where do you find a listing of appropriate telephone numbers?

2. How can you update weather reports and forecasts during flight?

3. If your destination does not issue a terminal aerodrome forecast, how can you determine the forecast weather at your ETA?

4. What is a PIREP? How significant is it? [AIM, AC 00-45]

5. Plan a cross-country flight, obtain a complete weather briefing, and complete a navigation log.

6. Is the weather satisfactory for the planned flight? If not, could a change in routing or a delay in the planned departure time allow you to proceed with the flight?

7. If weather deteriorates enroute, what should you do?

8. If you encounter moderate to severe turbulence, is it advisable to slow the air- plane below what speed? Explain.

9. If you discover you are lost, what should you do?

AERONAUTICAL CHARTS AND AIRPORT OPERATIONS

To answer questions 1 through 20, have the student use the sectional chart appropriate to the local area. Select a controlled airport and an uncontrolled airport with an FSS on the field (if available) to answer the first 10 questions.

1. Provide at least 10 different items of information pertaining to the controlled airport.

2. Is Class D airspace designated around the controlled airport? If so, when is it in effect?

3. What is the minimum MSL altitude you can use to overfly a tower-controlled airport without establishing two-way communications with the control tower? [FAR 91.129, 91.159]

4. At what times is the control tower in operation at this airport?

5. If you cannot contact the control tower on the normal frequency, can you receive an airport advisory on the UNICOM frequency? Explain. [AIM]

6. What frequency should you use to obtain an airport advisory at the uncontrolled airport? [AIM]

7. What other frequencies can you use to communicate with the FSS?

8. What is the minimum weather required at the uncontrolled airport before you can land under VFR? [FAR 91.155, 91.157]

9. Assume that all attempts to contact the FSS at the uncontrolled field are unsuccessful because your communications radio is apparently inoperative. According to regulations, is it legal to enter the surrounding Class E airspace without establishing two-way radio communications? [FAR 91.155]

10. In this situation, what is the proper procedure for determining the runway in use? How do you enter the traffic pattern? Can you use ATC light signals? [FAR 91.127, AIM]

11. How are VORs, VORTACs, and VOR/DMEs identified on a sectional chart?

12. Are VOR radials aligned to magnetic or true north?

13. Locate an example of each of the following types of airspace and explain its lateral and vertical limits, as well as its significance to a VFR flight.
   ◊ Class D
   ◊ Class E
   ◊ Uncontrolled airspace (Class G)
   ◊ Restricted airspace
   ◊ Military operations area (MOA)
   ◊ Military training route (MTR)

14. Locate an MTR on the sectional chart. Explain all you can about the MTR, based on its designation.

15. Where can you obtain current temporary flight restrictions (TFRs)?

16. Obtain a current TFR and draw the airspace limits on the appropriate sectional or terminal chart.

17. What is a flight restricted zone (FRZ)?

18. What is an air defense identification zone (ADIZ)?

19. On the sectional chart, locate an airport within Class D airspace. If the weather at that airport is reported as IFR due to ground fog, would you need to establish two-way communications with the control tower to fly VFR through the lateral limits of this Class D airspace area at 6,000 feet AGL? [FAR 91.129, 91.155]

20. Assuming the airport is reporting a 600-foot ceiling and one-mile visibility, could you conduct a VFR flight to and from the airport? [FAR 61.89, 91.155, 91.157]

21. What are the VFR and special VFR weather minimums for Class D airspace? [FAR 91.155, 91.157]

22. Locate an obstruction on the sectional chart. Immediately adjacent to it are two numbers (one in parentheses). What is the significance of each number?

23. If the DME is tuned to a VOR facility, what indications can you expect from the DME?

24. Locate a maximum elevation figure (MEF). Explain its significance.

25. Explain proper control wheel positioning for crosswind taxiing.

26. Relative to directional control, what must you be aware of during takeoff in a strong crosswind?

27. Describe the symbols on an airport that indicate either left-hand or right-hand traffic patterns.

28. Discuss the different colors associated with airport lighting and what each represents.

COLLISION AVOIDANCE

1. Which aircraft has the right-of-way over all other aircraft? [FAR 91.113]

2. Two aircraft of the same category are converging at the same approximate altitude. Which aircraft has the right-of-way? [FAR 91.113]

3. If a glider and an airplane are approaching head-on, or nearly so, who has the right-of-way and what action should be taken? [FAR 91.113]

4. One aircraft is on final approach and the second is waiting to take off. Which aircraft has the right-of-way? [FAR 91.113]

POSTFLIGHT PROCEDURES

1. After landing, what procedures should you follow concerning the shutdown, parking, and securing of your airplane?

2. After shutdown, why is it important to make sure the ignition switch has been placed in the OFF position?

3. When should you refuel the airplane? What are some precautionary steps that you should take during refueling?

NIGHT OPERATIONS

1. What are the differences between scanning for aircraft at night and during the day? [AIM]

2. Why is it important to carry a flashlight at night?

3. Is it easier or more difficult to avoid obstructions at night? Explain.

4. Is weather easier or more difficult to avoid at night? Explain.

5. How is a night takeoff different from one performed during the day? Explain.

6. Is a night approach flown differently than one flown during the day? Explain any differences.

EMERGENCY OPERATIONS

1. What is the definition of the best or maximum glide speed? What is the best glide speed for your airplane?

2. What is the approximate glide ratio for your airplane.

3. Discuss the procedures to be used if a partial or complete engine failure occurs.

4. If an engine fire develops during flight, what steps should you follow?

5. What procedure should you use if an electrical fire occurs?

6. While in flight, you note that the oil pressure is low, but the oil temperature remains normal. Explain what action you would take in this situation.

7. During flight, the engine oil pressure suddenly drops to zero and the oil temperature begins to rise. Explain what has happened and what action you would take in this situation.

8. After takeoff, your engine suddenly stops at an altitude of 100 feet AGL. What action should you take?

APPENDIX ■ Presolo Exam Briefing

AERODYNAMICS

1. Discuss the aerodynamic factors associated with stalls and spins.
2. At what indicated airspeed will your airplane stall at maximum takeoff weight with flaps down and power off?
3. What increase in stall speed can you expect in a 60° bank in the clean configuration?
4. What is an accelerated stall, and when is it most likely to occur? What are the typical causes of a spin, and how do you recover?
5. If you are operating the airplane at a low airspeed with full power during a descent, what action should you take to arrest the descent? Why?
6. Explain ground effect and how you can take advantage of it during takeoff.

REGULATIONS AND THE AERONAUTICAL INFORMATION MANUAL

1. How wide is a Victor airway? [FAR 71.75]
2. What is the significance of 14,500 feet MSL in the classification of airspace?
3. What type of information is in the Aeronautical Information Manual?
4. At what time of day may you begin logging night flight time? [FAR 1.1, 61.51, 61.57]
5. At what time must you turn on the aircraft position lights? [FAR 91.209]
6. What are the recency of experience requirements to carry passengers at night in a particular category and class of aircraft? [FAR 61.57]
7. Must an airplane always be equipped with an emergency locator transmitter? If not, explain the exceptions. [FAR 91.207]
8. When must your passengers be supplied supplemental oxygen? When are you, as pilot in command, required to use oxygen? [FAR 91.211]
9. When are passengers required to wear safety belts and, if installed, shoulder harnesses? [FAR 91.107]
10. What is the minimum allowable flight altitude over a sparsely populated area? [FAR 91.119]
11. Under what circumstances is it legal to drop an object from an aircraft while in flight? [FAR 91.15]
12. Are flight plans required for VFR cross-country flight?
13. What are the pilot and equipment requirements for operation within Class B airspace? [FAR 91.131(b), 61.95].
14. What are the pilot and equipment requirements for operation within Class C airspace? [FAR 91.130]
15. Who may give a flight review? How often must you obtain one? [FAR 61.56]
16. For a private pilot, what are the restrictions to acting as pilot in command of an airplane with more than 200 horsepower? What about an airplane with retractable landing gear, flaps, and a controllable-pitch propeller? [FAR 61.31]

17. According to NTSB 830, what is an aircraft accident and when must it be reported? What is the difference between an accident and an incident? [NTSB 830.5]

INTERCEPTION

1. What are the three intercept phases? [AIM]
2. What steps must you immediately take upon interception? [AIM]
3. If you are intercepted and unable to establish radio communication, how can you advise the intercepting aircraft you are in distress? [AIM]

AEROMEDICAL FACTORS

1. Discuss the similarities and differences between hypoxia, hyperventilation, and carbon monoxide poisoning. What are the symptoms and effects for each condition and what corrective actions should you take in each case?
2. If a passenger exhibits symptoms that could be attributed to more than one condition, what should you do? [AIM]
3. What are the rules concerning the use of alcohol and the operation of an aircraft? [FAR 91.17]
4. Name several common medications that you should not take before or during a flight.
5. What is spatial disorientation, when is it most likely to occur, and what corrective action should you take if you become spatially disoriented?
6. What are the effects of fatigue on a pilot?

APPENDIX ■ **Presolo Exam Briefing**

APPENDIX ■ **Presolo Exam Briefing**

This is to Certify that

_____

is enrolled in the

Federal Aviation Administration

_____ course

approved _____

conducted by _____ .

_____
Chief Instructor

_____
Date of Enrollment

This is to certify that

_____

has succesfully completed all stages, tests, and course requirements and has graduated from the FEDERAL AVIATION ADMINISTRATION _____ course approved _____

conducted by _____

I certify the above statements are true.

_____
Chief Instructor

_____
School certificate number

_____
Date of graduation

The graduate has completed the cross-country training specified in FAR Part 141.

☐ Private Pilot Certification Course — Appendix B, Paragraphs 4 and 5

☐ Instrument Rating Course — Appendix C, Paragraph 4(c)(1)(ii)

☐ Commercial Pilot Certification Course — Appendix D, Paragraphs 4 and 5

☐ Other: _____